TWIGG *stitch*

A NEW TWIST ON **REVERSIBLE KNITTING**

VICKI TWIGG

INTERWEAVE
interweave.com

EDITOR ● Ann Budd
TECHNICAL EDITOR ● Lori Gayle
ART DIRECTOR ● Julia Boyles
BEAUTY PHOTOGRAPHY ● Joe Hancock
SWATCH/STEP PHOTOGRAPHY ● Ann Swanson
PHOTO STYLIST ● Allie Liebgott
HAIR & MAKEUP ● Kathy MacKay
DESIGN ● Brass Bobbin Creative
PRODUCTION ● Katherine Jackson

Interweave
A division of F+W Media, Inc.
4868 Innovation Drive
Fort Collins, CO 80525
interweave.com

Manufactured in China by RR Donnelley
Shenzhen

Library of Congress
Cataloging-in-Publication Data

Twigg, Vicki.

Twigg stitch : a new twist on
reversible knitting / Vicki Twigg.

pages cm.

Includes index.

ISBN 978-1-59668-822-3 (pbk)
ISBN 978-1-59668-823-0 (PDF)

1. Knitting—Patterns. I. Interweave Press.
II. Title.

TT820.T96 2014

746.43'2—dc23

2014007998

10 9 8 7 6 5 4 3 2 1

ACKNOWLEDGMENTS

To the memory of my Mother, who taught me to knit, worked out her own unique ways of doing things, and always encouraged my explorations . . .

My endless thanks to my family—Geoff, Cat, Stiv, and Pete, and to my family in England, particularly Zoë and Gill, for their constant encouragement.

Thanks to Anna and the many friends through my life who have encouraged me in so many ways.

My thanks to my friends at my local knitting store, Sister Arts Studio in Chicago, especially Donna Palicka, for encouragement, ideas, and suggestions. Thanks also to the growing number of knitters who have learned Twigg stitch, come up with various new ways of knitting it, and, in some cases, sparked ideas.

Profound gratitude goes to the team at Interweave who worked with me on this book and to Julie Luckasen who allowed us to use her house and shop, My Sister Knits, in Fort Collins, Colorado, for the photography.

CONTENTS

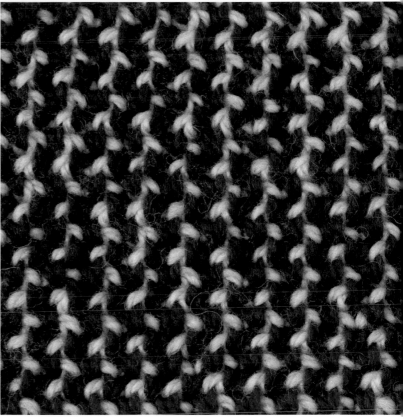

A TECHNIQUE IS BORN

I love to play around with unusual craft techniques, and I'm always on the lookout for interesting ones. Sometimes they find their way into the things that I'm making; sometimes they get filed away for another day, increasing the pile of remarkable samples in my box of ideas. Occasionally, my ideas cross-pollinate and team up with each other, sparking my imagination and sending me in a new direction of frenzied knitting or crochet or quilting—my family is accustomed to losing me to one of them every so often.

The inspiration for this particular stitch pattern happened in the fall of 2011. Looking at the structure of two-color rib, a technique in which the knit and purl stitches are different colors, set my mind working. I love the way the rib creates stripes that can be as dramatic or subtle as you want, and although it's not as stretchy as a regular rib, it makes a wonderful edging for various knitted projects. The only drawback I could see was that such two-color ribs look good on only one side because the color not in use is stranded behind the other stitches in the same way as "unused" yarns are stranded behind Fair Isle patterns.

I challenged myself to see if such ribs could be double-sided so that both front and back were equally beautiful. Having experimented over many years with various ways to use multiple yarns, I naturally began with a process similar to double knitting. In my efforts to make a single integrated fabric, I twisted the yarns around each other with every stitch. Although it felt as though I were holding the yarns "the wrong way," I continued and discovered what I was looking for—a two-sided rib fabric that was a different color on each side. I haven't found this technique anywhere in the literature, so I've named it Twigg stitch.

Basic Twigg stitch produces a two-color rib in which each side is a different color. It looks much the same as two-color brioche, but both colors are worked on every row and there are no slipped stitches or yarnovers. And, unlike double knitting, it produces a single fabric layer. The basics are fairly easy to learn and, once grasped, the possibilities are immense. After discovering Twigg stitch, I began endless experiments (which are still ongoing) to explore the limits of this two-color technique. It turns out that it can be applied in a variety of ways to other techniques, including cables, lace, colorwork, entrelac, and other texture patterns.

Twigg stitch uses familiar knitting skills and is easily learned by even novice knitters. It can be worked in the English (throwing) style as well as the Continental (picking) style of knitting, or by holding one yarn in each hand. Success lies largely in how the yarns are held and controlled—the key is in keeping them balanced and in the right relationship to each other.

Twigg Stitch isn't intended to be a how-to-knit book—many good resources are already available for those wanting to start knitting. I assume a basic knowledge of knitting and knitting terms, but at the same time, I've taken care to make the patterns accessible to knitters of all levels.

I hope you'll become as fascinated with the technique as I am, and that you'll find ways to use Twigg stitch in your own designs.

MATERIALS

As for any other knitting technique, the yarn and tools you choose will influence your success with Twigg stitch. The materials outlined in this chapter will facilitate your progress and ensure the best results.

Yarn

So many yarns are available to knitters now that the choices can be bewildering. The yarns that I used for each pattern have specific qualities that enhance the design. I tend to use relatively lightweight yarns for Twigg stitch because the two-strand nature of the stitch creates a fabric that's a little thicker. In many cases, another yarn of the same weight can be substituted quite successfully. But it's important to realize that the type of fiber used and how a yarn is constructed can have dramatic effects. You'll only know if a substitute is appropriate by knitting a sample swatch. I encourage you to experiment with various types of yarns to see how they behave in different projects and determine which you like best.

Keep in mind that texture can affect the overall look of Twigg stitch. For the most part, slipperier yarns will produce the most uniform fabric because they settle into the stitches. Clingy yarns may require a bit of adjustment—simply pulling on the fabric widthwise and lengthwise may do the trick. But if it doesn't, you might need to use a needle tip to adjust the stitches for a uniform look.

Although I've used different colors of the same yarn for each of the projects in this book, you can get interesting results by pairing different yarns. For the most even fabric, choose two yarns of similar thickness. However, you also can get pleasing results if one yarn is slightly thicker than the other or if you pair a smooth yarn with a slightly nubby one—provided you can achieve balanced stitches.

On a more practical note, you may want to pair an expensive specialty yarn with a cheaper plain one to cut costs while maintaining luxury. For example, you can use a yarn that contains sequins or beads for the "right" side and a plain yarn for the "wrong" side. Working the "lining" with a complementary yarn will keep all the finery on the outside and provide a visual surprise when the inside is visible. In addition, consider pairing yarns made from different fibers to take advantage of the characteristics of each. For example, wool will add stability and resilience to silk or alpaca; cotton will add next-to-the-skin softness to a scratchier yarn.

Color

Your choice of color will play a big role in the success of Twigg stitch. I've been surprised at how some combinations that I thought would look great turned out to be less than exciting and how others that I didn't think would work well turned out beautifully. The only way to be sure about how two colors will interact is to knit a swatch. I typically knit several swatches to find a combination of colors that come alive in the knitting.

Some of my favorite combinations involve two shades of the same color—such as the Fan Shawl on page 78 and the swatches in Chapter 4. But be aware that if you choose colors that are too similar, they may read as a single color and result in little visual difference between the two faces of the fabric. You can generally expect success if you pair a variegated yarn with a solid yarn, pair complementary colors, or use your favorite team colors. For additional combination ideas, see the subtle variations in the yarns used for the Lake Shore Wrap on page 54 and how two variegated yarns were used with success for the Brooke Beret on page 64.

Needles

Most knitters build large collections of needles that include an assortment of styles and types. Try them all to see what you like best for Twigg stitch. You may find that the needles you prefer for regular knitting may not work the same for Twigg stitch. Depending on the yarn you use and the way you choose to hold it, you may prefer needles with sharper or rounder points or needles with smoother or rougher surfaces when working Twigg stitch.

In general, I like to use metal needles for Twigg stitch because the stitches slide so easily on them. However, I also like the feel and lightness of bamboo when I use double-pointed needles, particularly when working small areas of shaping. No matter what type of needle you prefer, I recommend that you invest in the highest quality that you can afford. Needles are necessary tools for knitting, and you want them to work with you, not against you.

When you choose needle size, begin with the size recommended on the yarn ball band to get a feel for what the manufacturer suggests. From there, you can choose larger needles for a softer, lacy effect or smaller needles for a denser fabric. I've found that the stitches become uniform and the knitting becomes comfortable when I hit upon the perfect combination of needles, yarn, and the way that I tension the two colors.

Notions

In terms of notions, Twigg stitch is the same as regular knitting. I like to use removable stitch markers that can be placed and removed at any time. I use them to block off pattern repeats and to hold small numbers of stitches.

For weaving in ends, I like to use a sharp-point needle, such as a chenille needle, that has a larger eye than a typical sewing needle.

When I need to put stitches onto a holder, I generally use a smaller spare circular needle instead of a proper stitch holder. The stitches are safe on the cable portion and the tips hang out of the way. When it's time to work the held stitches again, it's a simple matter to slide them to the tip and work from there.

2 TWIGG-STITCH TECHNIQUES

Just like any other type of knitting, Twigg stitch involves specific techniques. Practice the techniques explained in this chapter before you embark on a project. You'll have the best results if you use two colors of the same smooth yarn while learning the techniques.

Basic Twigg Stitch

As with any kind of knitting, you can hold the yarn a variety of ways for the same result. You can work Twigg stitch while holding both yarns in your right hand, both yarns in your left hand, or one yarn in each hand. However you hold the yarn, be careful to keep the yarns in the correct position in relation to each other so that they twist after every stitch. To do so, you'll need to tension both yarns simultaneously as you knit; you can't drop one yarn while you work with the other.

If you can, I recommend holding (and tensioning) both yarns in the same hand—either the right or left. Doing so will ensure that the same amount of yarn is used for the knit and purl stitches, which is necessary for even tension. However, some patterns require different amounts of the two colors and, for these patterns, it's best to tension the two yarns in separate hands. I find that the way that I choose to hold the yarn depends on the stitch pattern and the type of yarn. It's therefore a good idea to become comfortable with at least two methods—holding one yarn in each hand and holding both yarns in the same hand.

If you're already accustomed to holding one yarn in each hand for Fair Isle patterns, that method will probably be the easiest for you to use while learning Twigg stitch. But keep an eye on the balance between the yarns—the purl stitches have a tendency to take up more yarn and result in uneven stitches from row to row. If you've never worked with a yarn in each hand, try holding both in the hand you typically use to tension single-yarn knitting as you learn this technique. Then try other tensioning methods as you gain confidence.

To begin, use one color of yarn and your favorite method (ribbed cable method shown here) to cast on an even number of stitches. Tie the other color onto the cast-on edge a few stitches in from the selvedge so you can tension both yarns equally.

Tie the second yarn to the cast-on edge a few stitches in from the selvedge.

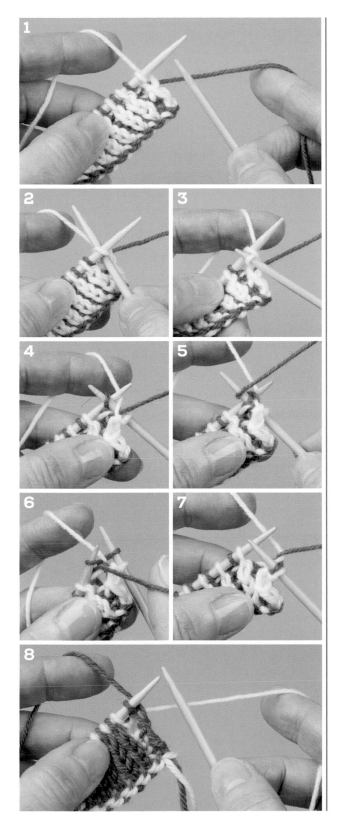

Holding One Yarn in Each Hand

Hold A (light), which will be used for the knit stitches, in your left hand, and hold B (dark), which will be used for the purl stitches, in your right hand (**Photo 1**).

With this method, your right hand does all the work, bringing the purl yarn to the front for the purl stitches and to the back for the knit stitches.

STEP 1: With both yarns at the back, insert the right needle tip knitwise into the knit stitch (**Photo 2**) and knit it with A (**Photo 3**).

Doing so forms a Twigg-knit stitch (abbreviated Tk).

STEP 2: Bring B to the front, take the right needle behind A to insert it purlwise into the purl stitch (**Photo 4**), and purl it with B (**Photos 5 and 6**), trapping A as you do so (it doesn't matter if A is behind or in front of the left needle). Bring B to the back (**Photo 7**).

Doing so forms a Twigg-purl stitch (abbreviated Tp).

Repeat Steps 1 and 2 to the end of the row.

Turn the knitting around and work with the opposite colors for the next row—hold B in your left hand for the knit stitches and hold A in your right hand for the purl stitches (**Photo 8**). For now, it doesn't matter which way you change the colors between rows, but you'll eventually want to follow the instructions for tidy selvedges on page 40.

Holding Both Yarns in Your Right Hand

Hold both yarns in your right hand (it's helpful to anchor them around your little finger) so that A (light), which will be used for the knit stitches, is on your middle finger and B (dark), which will be used for the purl stitches, is on your index finger (**Photo 1**). Be sure to maintain this separation as you knit.

STEP 1: With both yarns at the back, insert the right needle tip knitwise into the knit stitch (**Photo 2**) and knit it with A (**Photo 3**).

Doing so forms a Twigg-knit stitch (abbreviated Tk).

STEP 2: Bring both yarns to the front between the needles, insert the right needle tip purlwise into the purl stitch (**Photo 4**) and purl it with B, bringing B in front of A (**Photo 5**) so that the two yarns cross. Bring both yarns to the back (**Photo 6**).

Doing so forms a Twigg-purl stitch (abbreviated Tp).

Repeat Steps 1 and 2 to the end of the row.

Turn the knitting around and work with the opposite colors for the next row—hold B, which will be used for the knit stitches, over your middle finger and hold A, which will be used for the purl stitches, over your index finger (**Photo 7**). For now, it doesn't matter which way you change the colors between rows, but you'll eventually want to follow the instructions for tidy selvedges on page 40.

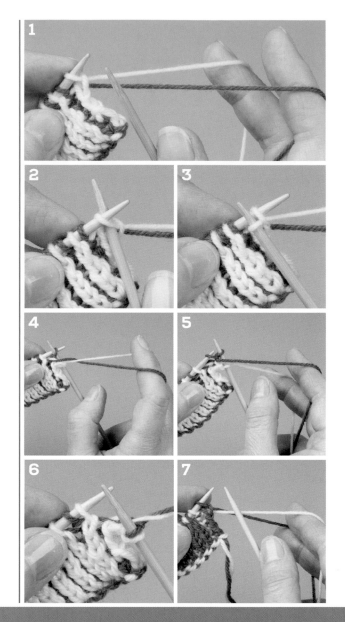

TWIGG-STITCH TIPS

The two yarns twist around each other in alternate directions after every stitch—these twists are essential for Twigg stitch. The way that you hold the yarn—both yarns in the right hand, both yarns in the left hand, or one yarn in each hand—can affect your gauge. ● Different types of needles may affect your ease of knitting and gauge—experiment to see what works best for the project at hand. ● Give yourself time to practice. Although Twigg stitch uses techniques you're used to, it's a new way to think about knitting. With practice, your fingers will learn the motions and you won't have to concentrate as much. ● Knit with firm tension to keep a balance between the two yarns. If necessary, hold the purl yarn more firmly to prevent the purl stitches from taking up more yarn, which will result in

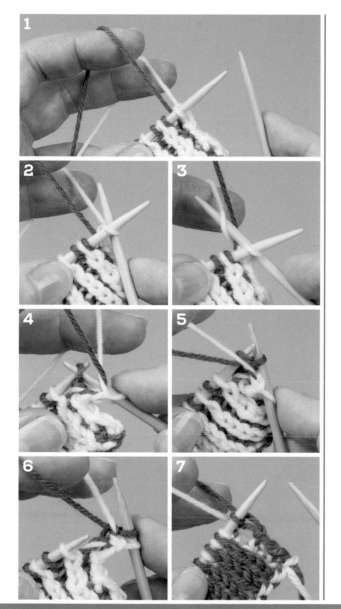

Holding Both Yarns in Your Left Hand

Hold both yarns in your left hand (it's helpful to anchor them around your little finger) so that A (light), which will be used for the knit stitches, is on your middle finger and B (dark), which will be used for the purl stitches, is on your index finger (**Photo 1**). Be sure to maintain this separation as you knit.

STEP 1: With both yarns at the back, insert the right needle tip knitwise into the knit stitch (**Photo 2**), bring the needle to the left of B and knit it with A (**Photo 3**).

Doing so forms a Twigg-knit stitch (abbreviated Tk).

STEP 2: With both yarns at the front, bring the right needle tip behind both yarns, insert it purlwise into the purl stitch (**Photo 4**) and purl it with B (**Photo 5**) so that B crosses in front of A. Bring both yarns to the back (**Photo 6**).

Doing so forms a Twigg-purl stitch (abbreviated Tp).

Repeat Steps 1 and 2 to the end of the row.

Turn the knitting around and work with the opposite colors for the next row—hold B, which will be used for the knit stitches, over your middle finger and hold A, which will be used for the purl stitches, over your index finger (**Photo 7**). For now, it doesn't matter which way you change the colors between rows, but you'll eventually want to follow the instructions for tidy selvedges on page 40.

uneven rows. ● For tidy selvedges, be consistent with how you manage the two yarns at the beginning of rows. See page 40 for options. ● Although the stitches on the row just below the needle may look a little loose or uneven, don't be tempted to change your knitting—they most likely will even out after another row or two. ● In the inevitable event that you need to stop in the middle of a row, bring the purl yarn to the front and the knit yarn to the back, then slide the stitches away from the needle points to ensure that the yarns are in the proper locations when you resume knitting. ● In general, Twigg stitch takes up to 50 percent more yarn than regular stockinette stitch; for most patterns, the total amount of yarn is divided equally between the two colors.

Cast-Ons

Many cast-ons are appropriate for Twigg stitch, whether you want a single-color or a two-color edge. The key is that the cast-on must produce an even number of stitches.

Single-Color Methods

All of the following methods work well for casting on stitches in a single color for Twigg stitch. To anchor the second color, tie it to the cast-on edge a few stitches from the selvedge (see page 10). You can pick out the knot later and weave in the ends for a clean finish.

> **note:** These methods are shown using the dark yarn, while the swatches (above) were worked with the light yarn.

CABLE CAST-ON

To begin, place a slipknot on the left needle to anchor the yarn, then use the **e-wrap method** to cast on another stitch (**Photo 1**)—two stitches on the left needle tip.

*Insert the right needle tip from front to back (knitwise) between the first two stitches on the left needle (**Photo 2**), pull the yarn to tension the stitch just made, wrap the yarn around the right needle knitwise (**Photo 3**), pull this loop to the front (**Photo 4**), and place it on the left needle in front of the last stitch made (**Photo 5**).

Repeat from * for the desired number of stitches, not counting the slipknot, which will be dropped from the needle on the first row of knitting.

Secure the last stitch as described on page 16.

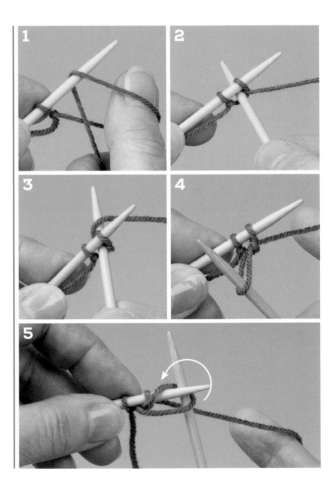

Ribbed Cable Cast-On, light side ◄ | ► *Ribbed Cable Cast-On, dark side*

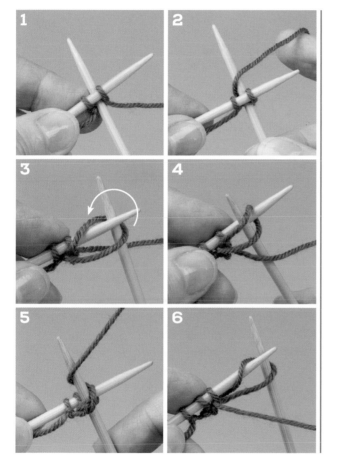

RIBBED-CABLE CAST-ON

The first step of this method creates the knit stitches and is the same as the regular cable cast-on. The second step creates the purl stitch. This is the same for knitting flat in rows or in rounds and looks the same on both sides.

Begin as for the cable cast-on by placing a slipknot on the left needle to anchor the yarn, then using the e-wrap method to cast on another stitch—two stitches on left needle tip.

STEP 1: With the working yarn in back, insert the right needle tip from front to back (knitwise) between the two stitches on the left needle (**Photo 1**), pull the yarn to tension the stitch just made, wrap the yarn around the right needle knitwise (**Photo 2**), pull this loop to the front, and place it on the left needle in front of the last stitch made (**Photo 3**).

This step forms a knit stitch on the needle.

STEP 2: With the working yarn in front, insert the right needle tip from back to front (purlwise) between the first two stitches on the left needle (**Photo 4**), pull the yarn to tension the last stitch made, wrap the yarn around the right needle purlwise (**Photo 5**), pull this loop to the back, and place it on the left needle in front of the last stitch made (**Photo 6**).

This step forms a purl stitch on the needle.

Repeat Steps 1 and 2 for the desired number of stitches, not counting the slipknot (which will be dropped from the needle on the first row of knitting), and ending with Step 1 (a knit stitch).

Secure the last stitch as described on page 16.

Long-Tail Cast-On, light side ◀ ▶ *Long-Tail Cast-On, dark side*

LONG-TAIL CAST-ON

> **note:** To determine the length of the tail, measure the length of yarn needed to wrap around the needle twenty times, then allow that length for every twenty stitches.

Leaving the necessary length of tail, hold the yarn in your left hand so that the tail end goes over your thumb and the ball end goes over your index finger. Secure the yarn ends with your other fingers, then insert the needle under the strand between your thumb and index finger slingshot fashion (**Photo 1**).

*Bring the needle from front to back (knitwise) up through the loop on your thumb (**Photo 2**), catch the first strand around your index finger (**Photo 3**), and bring the needle back down through the loop on your thumb (**Photo 4**). Drop the loop off your thumb (**Photo 5**) and tighten the stitch just formed on the needle.

Replace the yarn around your thumb as before and repeat from * for the desired number of stitches.

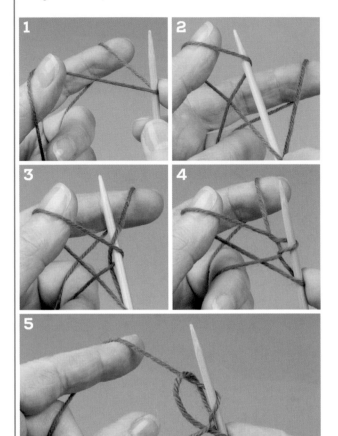

SECURE THE LAST CAST-ON STITCH

The base of the last stitch cast on using a cable method will not have a foundation (**Photo 1**). To secure this stitch, knit it (**Photo 2**), pull forward on the needle to tighten the knot at the base of the stitch (**Photo 3**), then return this new stitch to the left needle tip so that the leading leg of the loop is on the front of the needle (**Photo 4**) and the last stitch is secured (**Photo 5**).

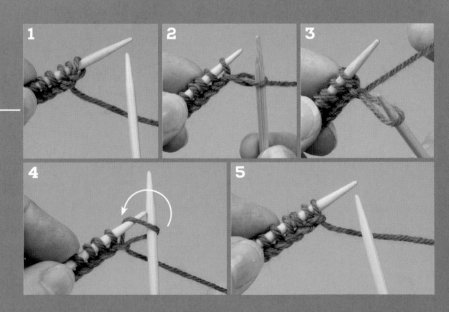

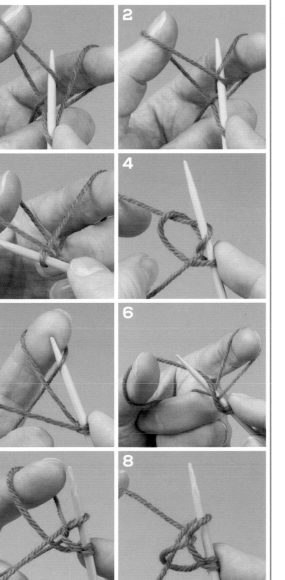

RIBBED LONG-TAIL CAST-ON

This method is worked in two steps to alternate knit and purl stitches. The first step is the same as the regular long-tail method.

> **note:** To determine the length of the tail, measure the length of yarn needed to wrap around the needle twenty times, then allow that length for every twenty stitches, plus a little for insurance.

Leaving the necessary length of tail, hold the yarn in your left hand so that the tail end goes over your thumb and the ball end goes over your index finger. Secure the yarn ends with your other fingers, then insert the needle under the strand between your thumb and index finger slingshot fashion as for the regular long-tail cast-on.

STEP 1: Bring the needle from front to back (knitwise) up through the loop on your thumb (**Photo 1**), catch the first strand around your index finger (**Photo 2**), then bring the needle back down through the loop on your thumb (**Photo 3**). Drop the loop off your thumb (**Photo 4**) and tighten the stitch just formed on the needle.

This step is the same as the regular long-tail cast-on and forms a knit stitch on the needle; it will be purled on the first row of knitting.

STEP 2: Bring the needle from back to front (purlwise) up through the loop on your index finger (**Photo 5**), scoop under the nearest strand around your thumb (**Photo 6**), then bring the needle back through the loop on your finger and away from you (**Photo 7**). Drop the loop off your finger (**Photo 8**) and tighten the stitch just formed on the needle.

This step forms a purl stitch on the needle; it will be knitted on the first row of knitting.

Repeat Steps 1 and 2 until you have one more than the desired number of stitches, ending with Step 2.

Decrease the extra stitch by Twigg-purling two stitches together (Tp2tog) at the end of the first row if working in rows or by Twigg-knitting two stitches together (Tk2tog) at the beginning of the first round if working in rounds.

Two-Color Methods

To work a two-color cast-on, begin by making a slipknot with A and B held together and place it on a needle held in your left hand. This slipknot anchors the yarns during the cast-on but will be removed on the first row of knitting.

In all cases, A will be used for the knit stitches on the first row of knitting.

Continue with your choice of the following options.

TWINED-CABLE CAST-ON

This two-color variation of the cable method causes the yarns to twist with every stitch; you'll need to untwist the yarns before you begin knitting.

Be careful not to tension the yarn too tightly, so you'll be able to fit the needle in the stitches on the first row of knitting.

STEP 1: With B (dark), use the e-wrap method to cast on one stitch next to the two-color slipknot, insert the right needle from front to back (knitwise) between these two stitches (**Photo 1**), then pull on the yarn to tension the B stitch just made.

STEP 2: Drop B to the back of the work, pick up A (light) and bring it in front of B (**Photo 2**) to use the cable method (see page 14) to cast on one stitch with A, insert the right needle knitwise between the last two stitches (**Photo 3**), then pull on the yarn to tension the A stitch just made.

STEP 3: Drop A to the back of the work, pick up B and bring it in front of A (**Photo 4**) to use the cable method to cast on one stitch with B, insert the right needle knitwise between the last two stitches (**Photo 5**), then pull on the yarn to tension the B stitch just made.

Repeat Steps 2 and 3 for the desired number of stitches, ending with Step 2 (**Photo 6**).

To secure the last A stitch cast on, insert the right needle tip knitwise into the last A stitch (**Photo 7**), then knit that stitch with A (**Photo 8**). Tighten the stitch below it a bit, bring B to the front between the needles, then return the stitch to the left needle (**Photo 9**).

Braided-Cable Cast-On, light side ◄ ► *Braided-Cable Cast-On, dark side*

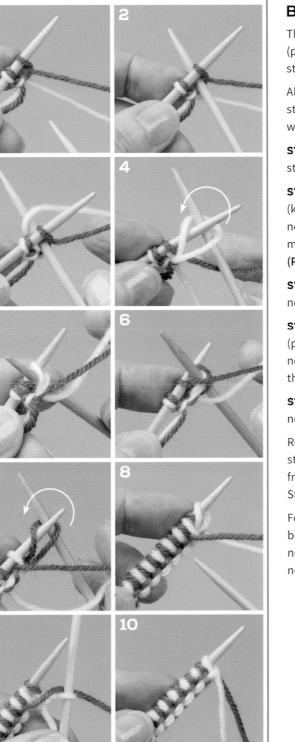

BRAIDED-CABLE CAST-ON

This method is similar to the ribbed-cable cast-on (page 15) but is worked with two colors so that the knit stitches are one color and the purl stitches are the other.

Always keep A (light), which will be used for the knit stitches, at the back of the work and keep B (dark), which will be used for the purl stitches, at the front of the work.

STEP 1: With B, use the e-wrap method to cast on one stitch next to the two-color slipknot, (**Photo 1**).

STEP 2: Insert the right needle tip from front to back (knitwise) between the first two stitches on the left needle (**Photo 2**), pull B to tension the B stitch just made, then wrap A knitwise around the right needle tip (**Photo 3**).

STEP 3: Pull this loop to the front and place it on the left needle in front of the previous B stitch (**Photo 4**).

STEP 4: Insert the right needle tip from back to front (purlwise) between the first two stitches on the left needle (**Photo 5**), pull A to tension the A stitch just made, then wrap B purlwise around the right needle (**Photo 6**).

STEP 5: Pull this loop to the back and place it on the left needle in front of the previous A stitch (**Photo 7**).

Repeat Steps 2 through 5 for the desired number of stitches, not counting the slipknot (which will be dropped from the needle on the first row of knitting), ending with Step 3 (a knitwise stitch; **Photo 8**).

For a tidy finish, knit one stitch with A, tighten the stitch below it a bit, then bring B to the back between the two needles (**Photo 9**) and place the new A stitch on the left needle tip (**Photo 10**).

SLIMLINE-CABLE CAST-ON

This method has less stretch then other cable cast-ons, so you may want to work it with needles one size larger than you plan to use for the project. Work with A (light) at the front of the work and B (dark) at the back.

STEP 1: With B, use the e-wrap method to cast on one stitch next to the two-color slipknot, insert the right needle tip from front to back (knitwise) between these two stitches (**Photo 1**), then pull on the yarn to tension the B stitch just made.

STEP 2: Bring A in front of B, then use the cable method (see page 14) to cast on one stitch knitwise with A (**Photo 2**). Insert the right needle tip from back to front (purlwise) between the first two stitches on the left needle (**Photo 3**), then pull the yarn to tension the A stitch just made.

STEP 3: Bring B around A (**Photo 4**) to use the cable method to cast on one stitch purlwise (**Photo 5**).

Repeat Steps 2 and 3 for the desired number of stitches plus one, not counting the slipknot (which will be dropped from the needle on the first row of knitting), ending with a purl (B) stitch; the A yarn will be a few stitches from the end of the needle (**Photo 6**).

For a tidy finish, slip the last (B) stitch to the right needle (**Photo 7**), bring A to the back between the needles (**Photo 8**), then slip the B stitch back onto the left needle (**Photo 9**). At the beginning of the first row, k2tog with A (**Photo 10**).

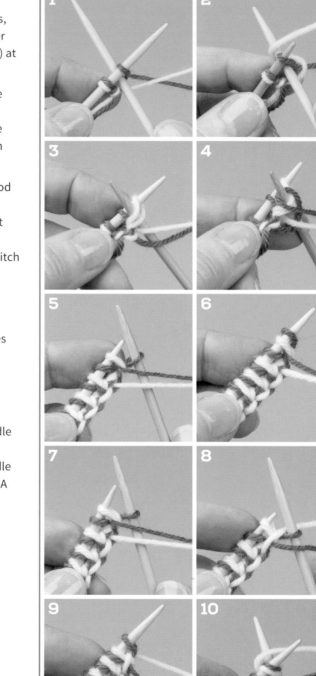

Two-Color Ribbed Long-Tail Cast-On, light side ◄ | ► *Two-Color Ribbed Long-Tail Cast-On, dark side*

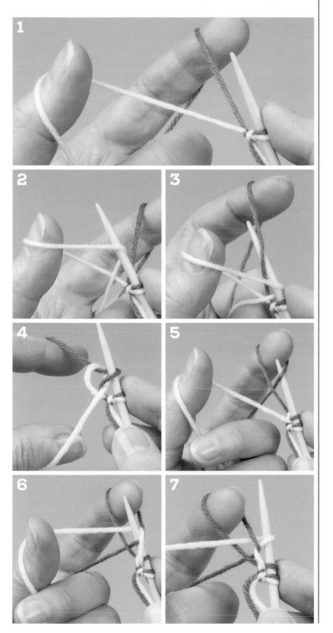

TWO-COLOR RIBBED LONG-TAIL CAST-ON

This method is worked the same as the single-color ribbed long-tail cast-on (see page 17), but different colors of yarn are held over the thumb and index finger. Make a slipknot of two colors held together and place it on a needle held in your right hand. Hold the yarns in your left hand as for the single-color method so that A (light) makes a loop over your thumb and B (dark) makes a loop over your index finger (**Photo 1**). Secure the yarns with your other fingers.

STEP 1: Bring the needle from front to back (knitwise) up through the A loop on your thumb (**Photo 2**), catch the first B strand (**Photo 3**), and bring the needle back down through the loop on your thumb. Drop the loop off your thumb (**Photo 4**) and tighten the B stitch just formed on the needle.

This forms a knit stitch as you view it; it will be purled on the first row of knitting.

STEP 2: Bring the needle from back to front (purlwise) through the B loop on your index finger (**Photo 5**), scoop under the nearest A strand (**Photo 6**), then bring the needle to the back through the loop on your index finger (**Photo 7**). Drop the B loop off your index finger and tighten the A stitch just formed on the needle.

This forms a purl stitch as you view it; it will be knitted on the first row of knitting.

Repeat Steps 1 and 2 for the desired number of stitches.

If working in rounds, hold the desired knit color over your index finger and the desired purl color over your thumb.

ITALIAN CAST-ON

In addition to creating a foundation row of Twigg stitch, this cast-on method forms a very flexible and elastic edge with well-balanced stitches.

STEP 1: With smooth waste yarn (cotton is best) and a crochet hook a couple of sizes larger than the needles you plan to use, make a crochet chain about six stitches longer than the desired number of stitches. End by pulling the last stitch into a large loop (**Photo 1**; you'll use this loop to identify the end to pull on to remove the waste yarn). Turn the chain over and, beginning and ending about three stitches from the ends of the chain, insert the knitting needle from front to back (**Photo 2**) into the back loop of each crochet stitch, taking care that the loops are mounted properly with the leading leg at the front of the needle (**Photo 3**).

STEP 2: Make a slipknot with A and B held together (this slipknot anchors the yarns during the cast-on but will be removed on the first row of knitting) and place it on the right needle (**Photo 4**).

STEP 3: Using A (light) for the knit stitches and B (dark) for the purl stitches, alternate Twigg-knit and Twigg-purl stitches (dropping the slipknot off the needle when you come to it at the end of the second row (**Photo 5**).

After several rows have been worked, remove the waste yarn by pulling on the open loop of the crochet chain (**Photo 6**) and drawing the waste yarn through the base of the cast-on edge (**Photo 7**). Pull out the two-color slipknot (**Photo 8**).

You can use this method to add two or more stitches to an existing row of knitting. Simply make a crochet chain the necessary length and work across the extra stitches at the end of the row.

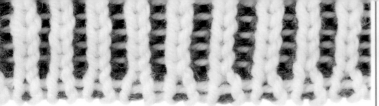

Two-Color Tubular Cast-On, light side ◄ | ► *Two-Color Tubular Cast-On, dark side*

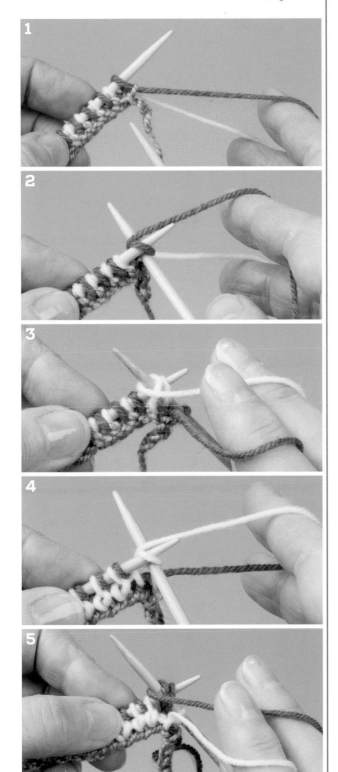

TWO-COLOR TUBULAR CAST-ON

With smooth waste yarn, provisionally cast on the desired number of stitches and work one row in Twigg stitch as described for the Italian method on page 22 (**Photo 1**).

Then work one or two set-up rows in double knitting as follows, holding the yarn for the knit stitches in front and the yarn for the purl stitches in back to prevent them from twisting around each other. In this example, B (dark) forms the knit stitches and A (light) forms the purl stitches on the first row; the colors are reversed for the second row.

SET-UP ROW 1: Holding both yarns in back, *k1 with B (**Photo 2**), bring both yarns to the front between the needles and p1 with A (**Photo 3**), bring both yarns to the back between the needles; repeat from *.

SET-UP ROW 2: Switch the way that the yarns are held so that the yarn for the knit stitches is held in back and the yarn for the purl stitches is held in front. Holding both yarns in back, *k1 with A (**Photo 4**), bring both yarns to the front between the needles and p1 with B (**Photo 5**), bring both yarns to the back between the needles; repeat from * to the slipknot. Drop the slipknot off the needle.

Continue in Twigg stitch, working the stitches and colors as they appear.

MÖBIUS CAST-ON

This cast-on is quite similar to the method introduced by Cat Bordhi in *A Second Treasury of Magical Knitting* (Passing Paws Press, 2005). You'll need a circular needle that's at least 40" (100 cm) long, and you'll need to cast on enough stitches to span at least 20" (51 cm) in width.

STEP 1: Make a slipknot with both yarns held together and place it on the left needle tip (this slipknot anchors the yarns for the cast-on and will be removed later). Slide the left needle tip toward the right so that the slipknot is on the cable behind the needle (**Photo 1**) and the cable is below the right needle tip, and hold the yarns as for the long-tail method with your left hand around the cable, A (light) over your index finger, and B (dark) over your thumb (**Photo 2**).

STEP 2: To make a knit stitch on the needle, bring the right needle tip to the front, then under B and the cable (**Photo 3**), then over the top of A to grab a stitch (**Photo 4**).

STEP 3: To complete the stitch, bring the needle back under B and the cable, then to the front so that B and the cable are below the needle (**Photo 5**).

STEP 4: To make a purl stitch on the needle, bring the needle over the top of and then behind A, the cable, and B (**Photo 6**), then over the top of B and to the back to form a B stitch on the needle. To complete the stitch, bring the needle to the back, behind the cable and A, then up so that the cable and A are below the right needle (**Photo 7**).

Repeat Steps 2 through 4 for the desired number of stitches, maintaining even, but not tight, tension on the two yarns. You may want to use markers to help count the stitches, but try not to let go of the yarns until all the stitches have been cast on.

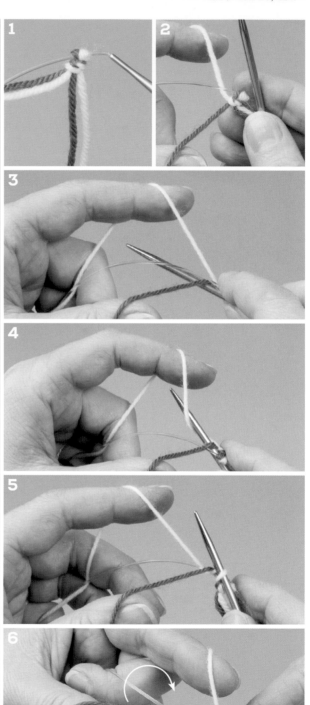

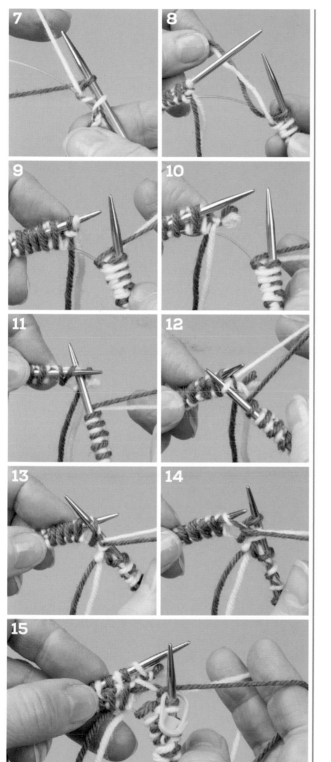

▶ Möbius Cast-On, back

STEP 5: To finish, bring both yarns to the front, over the cable, and to the back in position to work the first round (**Photo 8**), then slide the stitches around the doubled cable loop so that the slipknot is on the left needle tip (**Photo 9**).

Drop the slipknot off the needle, but don't undo it so that the yarn tails hold together (**Photo 10**).

SET-UP RND: Tension the two yarns for Twigg stitch so that A (light) will be used for the knit stitches and B (dark) will be used for the purl stitches. The stitches will be mounted in alternating directions on the needles so that you'll need to work into the back loop of the knit stitches and into the front loop of the purl stitches. Each stitch will consist of a strand of each color.

*Starting with both yarns at the back, insert the right needle from front to back (knitwise) under the two yarns between the A and B stitches on the cable (**Photo 11**) and Twigg-knit with A (**Photo 12**), bring both yarns to the front between the needle tips, insert the right needle from back to front (purlwise) under the two yarns between the B and A stitches on the cable (**Photo 13**) and Twigg-purl with B (**Photo 14**); repeat from * to the slipknot, then place a marker to indicate the end of the round (**Photo 15**).

Note that each round involves knitting twice around the loop—once to work the stitches on the top and once to work the stitches on the bottom of the cast-on edge, so you have twice the original number of stitches on the needle.

Bind-Offs

These methods are all worked on knit-one-purl-one (k1, p1) ribbing that begins with a knit as the first stitch.

Single-Color Methods

VICKI'S SINGLE-COLOR RIBBED BIND-OFF

This method forms a zigzag edge that's as stretchy as the knitting. It's worked by knitting the purl stitches and purling the knit stitches.

STEP 1: Purl the first stitch (this will be the first knit stitch on the left needle; **Photo 1**), then with the yarn still in front, slip this stitch purlwise onto the left needle tip (**Photo 2**).

STEP 2: Bring the yarn to the back and slip the first two stitches individually knitwise (**Photo 3**), then knit them together through their back loops as for an ssk decrease (**Photo 4**).

STEP 3: Slip the resulting stitch purlwise onto the left needle tip (**Photo 5**), bring the yarn to the front and purl two stitches together as for a p2tog decrease (**Photo 6**), then slip the resulting stitch purlwise onto the left needle (**Photo 7**).

Repeat Steps 2 and 3.

To adapt this method for k2, p2 ribbing, work Step 2 every time you come to a purl stitch and work Step 3 every time you come to a knit stitch.

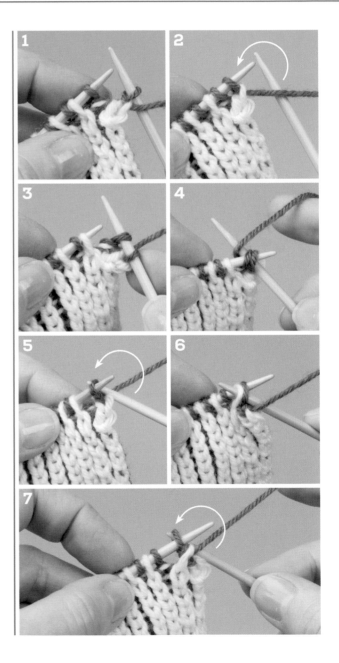

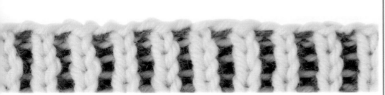

Ribbed-Chain Bind-Off, light side ◄ | ► *Ribbed-Chain Bind-Off, dark side*

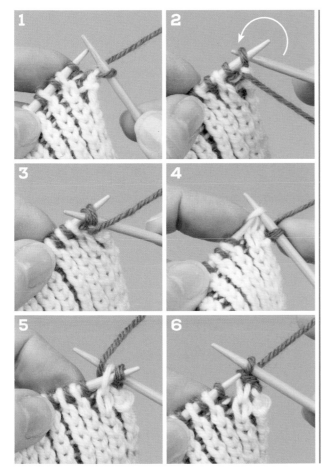

RIBBED-CHAIN BIND-OFF

This method makes a chain that sits along the top of the rib and looks the same from both sides. Take care not to work too tightly.

To begin, knit the first stitch (**Photo 1**).

STEP 1: Bring the yarn to the front between the needles, slip this stitch back onto the left needle tip (**Photo 2**), then purl the next two stitches together as for a p2tog decrease (**Photo 3**).

STEP 2: Bring the yarn to the back between the needles, slip the next stitch knitwise (**Photo 4**), insert the left needle tip into the front of these two stitches (**Photo 5**), then knit them together through their back loops as for a ssk decrease (**Photo 6**).

Repeat Steps 1 and 2 to the end of the row.

To adapt this method for k2,p2 ribbing, work Step 1 every time you come to a purl stitch and work Step 2 every time you come to a knit stitch.

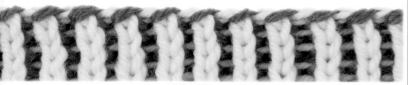

Two-Color Ribbed-Chain Bind-Off with Opposite Colors, light side ◄ ► *Two-Color Ribbed-Chain Bind-Off with Opposite Colors, dark side*

Two-Color Methods

TWO-COLOR RIBBED-CHAIN BIND-OFF

This method is the same as the single-color version but creates a chain of alternating colors along the bind-off edge. Depending on which yarn is held for the knit stitches and which yarn is held for the purl stitches, the bind-off stitches can be the opposite color or the same color as the stitches below. Be careful not to work too tightly.

With Opposite Colors

In this example, A (light) appears as knit stitches and B (dark) appears as purl stitches at the beginning of the bind-off row. The bind-off row will form B stitches on top of A stitches and form A stitches on top of B stitches.

Hold the yarns as for Twigg stitch with A for the knit stitches and B for the purl stitches.

To begin, Twigg-knit one stitch with A (**Photo 1**).

STEP 1: Bring both yarns to the front between the needles (**Photo 2**), slip the stitch just knitted to the left needle tip purlwise (**Photo 3**), then Twigg-purl the first two stitches together with B (**Photos 4 and 5**).

STEP 2: Bring both yarns to the back between the needles, slip one stitch knitwise to the right needle tip (there are now two stitches on the right needle; **Photo 6**), then insert the left needle tip into the fronts of these stitches and Twigg-knit them together through their back loops as for a ssk decrease with A (**Photo 7**).

Repeat Steps 1 and 2 to the end of the row.

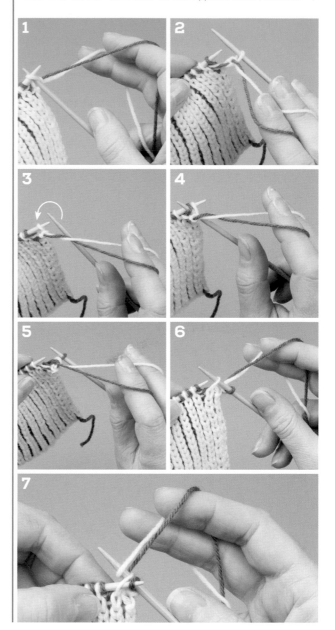

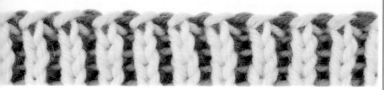

Two-Color Ribbed-Chain Bind-Off with Matching Colors, light side ◄

► *Two-Color Ribbed-Chain Bind-Off with Matching Colors, dark side*

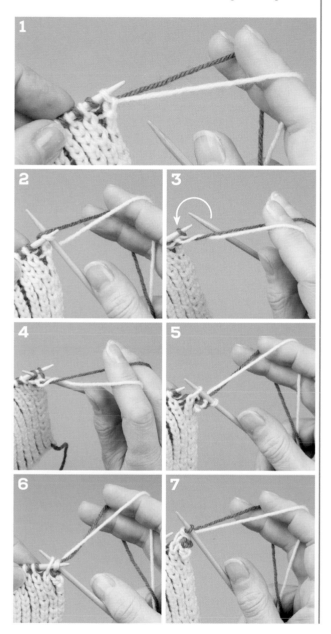

With Matching Colors

In this example, A (light) appears as the knit stitches and B (dark) appears as the purl stitches at the beginning of the bind-off row. The bind-off row will form A stitches on top of A stitches and form B stitches on top of B stitches.

Hold the yarns as for Twigg stitch the opposite of how you would normally hold them for this row of knitting so that B will be used for the knit stitches and A will be used for the purl stitches (**Photo 1**).

To begin, Twigg-knit one stitch with B (**Photo 2**).

STEP 1: Bring both yarns to the front between the needles, slip the stitch just knitted to the left needle tip purlwise (**Photo 3**), then Twigg-purl the first two stitches together with A (**Photo 4**).

STEP 2: Bring both yarns to the back between the needles, slip one stitch knitwise to the right needle tip (there are now two stitches on the right needle; **Photo 5**), then Twigg-knit these two stitches together through their back loops with B, as for a ssk decrease (**Photos 6 and 7**).

Repeat Steps 1 and 2 to the end of the row.

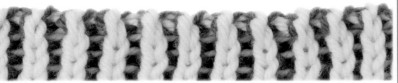

Vicki's Two-Color Ribbed Bind-Off, light side ◀ ▶ *Vicki's Two-Color Ribbed Bind-Off, dark side*

VICKI'S TWO-COLOR RIBBED BIND-OFF

This two-color version of my ribbed bind-off is also very stretchy.

This method is easiest if both yarns are held in your right hand. Hold A in the knit-yarn position and B in the purl-yarn position. You will, however, twist the yarns around each other as you work. Be careful not to tighten the stitches too much as you work.

To begin, purl the first stitch with A, slip this stitch back to the left needle tip, take A under B and to the back into the knit yarn position, then slip the first two stitches individually knitwise (**Photo 1**).

STEP 1: Ssk with B, bringing B behind A to twist the yarns (**Photos 2 and 3**), then return this stitch to the left needle tip.

STEP 2: P2tog with A (**Photo 4**), bringing A behind B to twist the yarns (**Photos 5 and 6**), then return this stitch to the left needle tip (**Photo 7**).

Repeat Steps 1 and 2 to the end of the row.

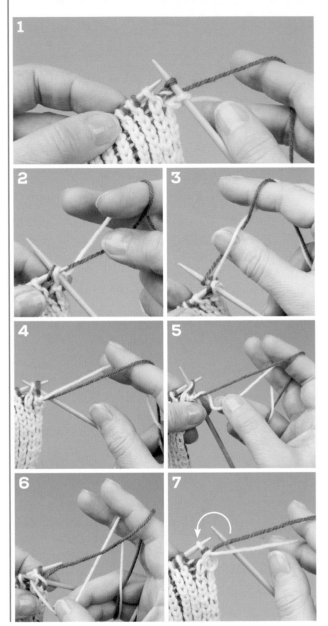

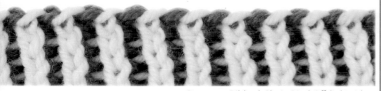

Decrease Ribbed-Chain Bind-Off, light side ◄ | ► *Decrease Ribbed-Chain Bind-Off, dark side*

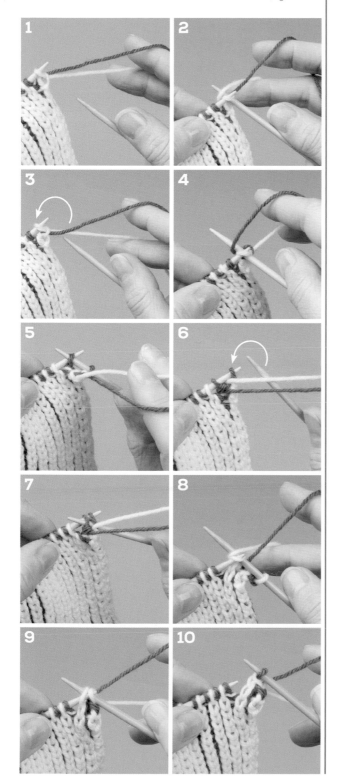

DECREASE RIBBED-CHAIN BIND-OFF

In this method, the stitches are bound off through a series of decreases. It looks the same as the two-color ribbed-chain bind-off worked with matching colors, but because each stitch is worked twice, it has much more inherent stretch.

Hold the yarns so that A will be used for the knit stitches and B will be used for the purl stitches (**Photo 1**).

To begin, Twigg-knit one stitch with A (**Photo 2**), return this stitch knitwise to the left needle tip (**Photo 3**), then knit the same stitch with B (**Photo 4**).

STEP 1: Bring both yarns to the front between the needles and Twigg-purl one stitch with B (**Photo 5**), return the two stitches to the left needle tip (**Photo 6**), then purl them together as usual with A (**Photo 7**).

STEP 2: Bring both yarns to the back between the needles and Twigg-knit one stitch with A (**Photo 8**), insert the left needle tip in the fronts of these two stitches (**Photo 9**), then knit them together through their back loops with B as for a ssk decrease (**Photo 10**).

Repeat Steps 1 and 2 to the end of the row.

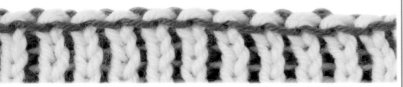

VICKI'S BRAIDED BIND-OFF

Hold the yarns so that A is in the knit position. Keep A at the back and B at the front and work with the right needle between the two yarns (**Photo 1**).

Be careful not to tighten the yarns as you work.

To begin, purl the first stitch (a knit stitch) with B (**Photo 2**).

STEP 1: Slip the next stitch knitwise (**Photo 3**), Twigg-knit two stitches together through the back loops with A as for a ssk decrease (**Photo 4**), then slip the resulting stitch purlwise to the left needle tip (**Photo 5**).

STEP 2: Purl two stitches together with B (**Photo 6**).

Repeat Steps 1 and 2 to the end of the row.

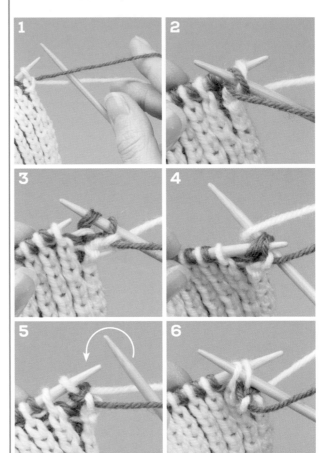

MATCHING CAST-ONS AND BIND-OFFS

When both the cast-on and bind-off edges of a piece are visible, it's pleasing if the two edges look the same. Several of the cast-on and bind-off methods described here—whether worked with a single color or two colors—have "matching" looks.

SINGLE-COLOR PAIRS

For identical looks, pair the single-color ribbed-cable cast-on (page 15) with Vicki's single-color ribbed bind-off (page 26), working one row of single-color rib before the bind-off to balance the look.

For a very similar look, pair the single-color ribbed long-tail cast-on (page 17) with Vicki's single-color ribbed bind-off (page 26).

TWO-COLOR PAIRS

For identical looks, pair the two-color slimline-cable cast-on (page 20) with the two-color slimline bind-off (page 33) or pair the Italian cast-on (page 22) with Vicki's two-color ribbed bind-off (page 30).

For a similar look, pair the twined-cable cast-on (worked loosely; page 18) with the decrease ribbed-chain bind-off (page 31) or pair the braided-cable cast-on (page 19) with Vicki's braided bind-off (page 32).

▶ *Slimline-Rib Bind-Off, light side* ◀ ▶ *Slimline-Rib Bind-Off, dark side*

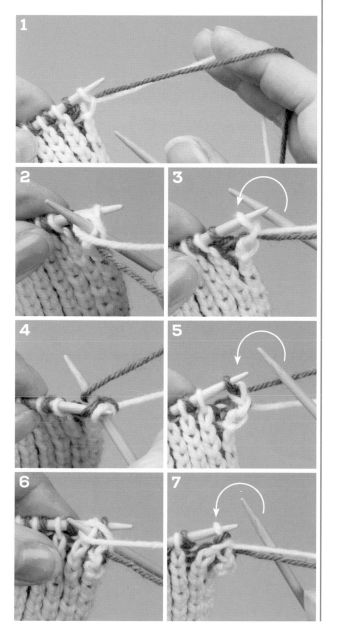

SLIMLINE-RIB BIND-OFF

Hold the yarns as you would for the next row, with A in the knit position and B in the purl position (**Photo 1**). However, you'll use them the other way around so that they cross over each other.

Be careful not to work too tightly; use needles one or two sizes larger if desired.

To begin, purl the first stitch (a knit stitch) with A (**Photo 2**), then slip this stitch purlwise to the left needle tip (**Photo 3**).

STEP 1: Bring both yarns to the back, ssk as usual with B, crossing B over A (**Photo 4**), then return the resulting stitch purlwise to the left needle tip (**Photo 5**).

STEP 2: Bring both yarns to the front, purl two stitches together as usual with A, crossing A over B (**Photo 6**), then return the resulting stitch to the left needle tip (**Photo 7**).

Repeat Steps 1 and 2 to the end of the row.

Decreases

When you decrease in Twigg stitch, keep in mind that stitches have to be worked in pairs to maintain the light-dark pattern of the knits and purls. That is, each decrease involves a knit stitch of one color and a purl stitch of the other color.

Symmetrical Decreases

This type of decrease eliminates a rib from each side of the fabric without interrupting the established pattern of the neighboring stitches.

SINGLE-RIB DECREASE

Work to one stitch (this will be a purl stitch) before the rib to be decreased (**Photo 1**), Twigg-purl two stitches together with the purl yarn (**Photo 2**), then Twigg-knit two stitches together with the knit yarn (**Photo 3**)—one stitch of each color (one rib) has been decreased (**Photo 4**).

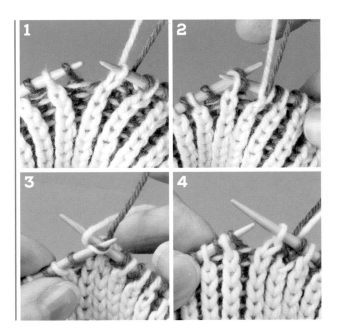

Right-Leaning Decrease (left) and Left-Leaning Decrease (right), light side ◄ | ► *Right-Leaning Decrease (left) and Left-Leaning Decrease (right), dark side*

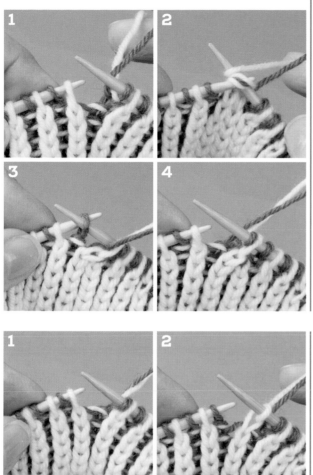

Directional Decreases

The following methods are worked over four stitches and create ribs that slant to one side. Note that a decrease that leans to the right on the light side of the fabric will lean to the left on the dark side and vice versa.

RIGHT-LEANING DECREASE

Work to the knit stitch (or rib) that you want to decrease (**Photo 1**), Twigg-knit three stitches together (two knit stitches plus the purl stitch between them) with the knit yarn (**Photo 2**), then Twigg-purl one stitch with the purl yarn (**Photo 3**)—one stitch of each color (one rib) has been decreased (**Photo 4**).

LEFT-LEANING DECREASE

Work to the knit stitch before the knit stitch (or rib) you want to decrease (**Photo 1**), Twigg-knit one stitch with the knit yarn (**Photo 2**), then Twigg-purl three stitches (two purl stitches plus the knit stitch between them) together with the purl yarn (**Photo 3**)—one stitch of each color (one rib) has been decreased (**Photo 4**).

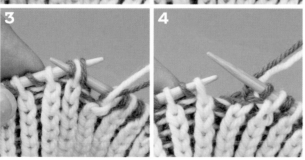

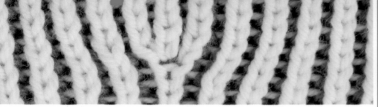

Double-Rib Decrease

This very easy method makes a centered double-rib decrease.

Work to the three ribs that you want to decrease into one, ending with a purl stitch (**Photo 1**), Twigg-knit three stitches (two knit stitches and the purl stitch between them) together as for k3tog (**Photo 2**), then Twigg-purl the next three stitches (two purl stitches and the knit stitch between them) together as for p3tog (**Photo 3**)— two stitches of each color (two ribs) have been decreased (**Photo 4**).

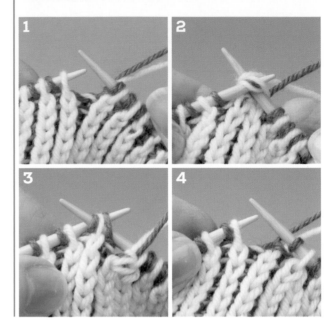

Increases

Just as for decreases, when you increase in Twigg stitch, keep in mind that the increases have to be worked in pairs to maintain the light-dark pattern of the knits and purls. That is, each increase involves a knit stitch of one color and a purl stitch of the other color.

Reverse Yarnover

This method, abbreviated "ryo," is worked as a backward yarnover over two rows. It keeps the two yarns together and makes it easier to work them together on the next row.

ROW 1: Work to the point at which you want the increase to appear, ending with a purl stitch, bring both yarns to the back between the two needles, then bring both yarns from back to front over the top of the right needle tip and between the two needles to the back again to create a double-strand loop with a reverse mount (**Photo 1**).

ROW 2: Twigg-knit into the back of the double-strand loop (**Photo 2**), then Twigg-purl into the back of the same double loop (**Photo 3**)—one stitch of each color has been increased (**Photo 4**).

Symmetrical Increases

This type of increase introduces a new rib on each side of the fabric without interrupting the established pattern of the neighboring stitches.

SINGLE-RIB INCREASE

Work to the point at which you want the new rib to begin, ending with a purl stitch, then use the left needle tip to pick up the pair of horizontal strands between the needles from front to back so that the knit yarn is to the right of the purl yarn (**Photo 1**), Twigg-knit the knit-color strand (**Photo 2**), then Twigg-purl the purl-color strand (**Photo 3**)—one stitch of each color (one rib) has been increased (**Photo 4**).

LIFTED INCREASE

This method is quite quick but leaves a slight hole at the base of the increase.

Work to the point at which you want the new rib to begin, ending with a purl stitch, then use the left needle tip to pick up the pair of horizontal strands between the needles from front to back (**Photo 1**), Twigg-knit both lifted strands with the knit yarn (**Photo 2**), then Twigg-purl both lifted strands with the purl yarn (**Photo 3**)—one stitch of each color (one rib) has been increased (**Photo 4**).

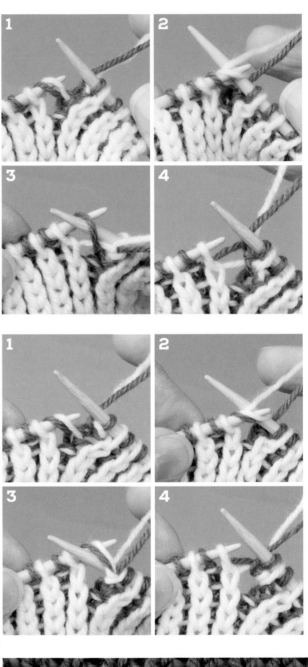

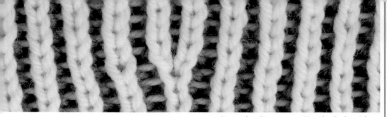

Branched Increase Single, light side ◄ ► *Branched Increase Single, dark side*

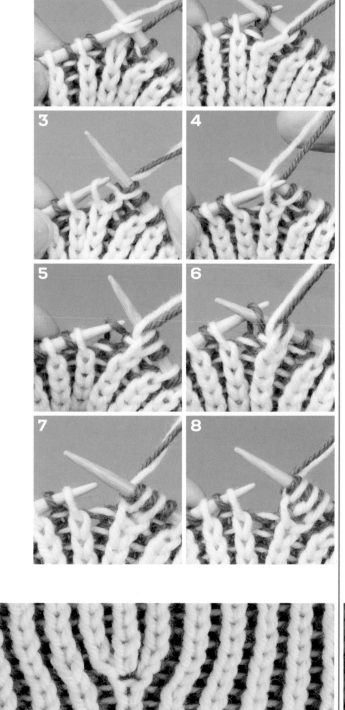

Branched Increase

This method involves knitting two (or three) times into the same two (or pair of) stitches. The result has a symmetrical look.

For a single-rib increase, work to the point at which you want the increase to occur, ending with a purl stitch, then Twigg-knit the knit stitch (**Photo 1**), Twigg-purl the purl stitch (**Photo 2**), *use the left needle to pick up the left leg of the stitch just knitted (**Photo 3**) and Twigg-knit it again (**Photo 4**), bring the yarns to the front and, working on the opposite side of the fabric, use the left needle tip to pick up the left leg of the purl stitch just worked (**Photo 5**), and Twigg-purl it again (**Photos 6 and 7**)—one stitch of each color (one rib) has been increased.

For a double-rib increase, repeat from * once (**Photo 8**)— two stitches of each color (two ribs) have been increased.

Branched Increase Double, light side ◄ ► *Branched Increase Double, dark side*

Knit Over Purl ◄   ► *Slip Stitch*

Selvedges

The way that you manipulate the two yarns when turning the work at the end of each row will affect the look of the selvedge edges. The method you choose can prevent stretching, create a decorative edge, or produce a foundation for picking up stitches or sewing reversible seams. Take time to experiment with the different methods to find the one that's best for your project. It's quite possible for the same technique to give different looks with different yarns.

The examples here are all based on ribbing that begins with a knit stitch.

KNIT OVER PURL

At the beginning of every row, bring the knit yarn over the purl yarn (**Photo 1**). This method forms alternating long and short stitches that prevent the edge from drawing in.

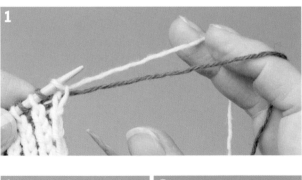

SLIP STITCH

Slip the first two stitches of every row purlwise, holding both yarns in the back while slipping the first stitch (**Photo 1**) and bringing both yarns forward between the needles to slip the second stitch (**Photo 2**). Bring both yarns to the back between the needles to work the next stitch. This method forms a tidy selvedge that doesn't stretch.

Garter Stitch (knit over purl) ◄ | ► Garter Stitch (knit under purl)

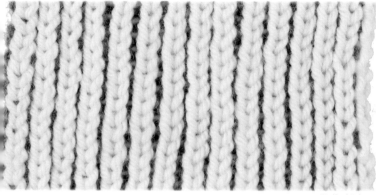

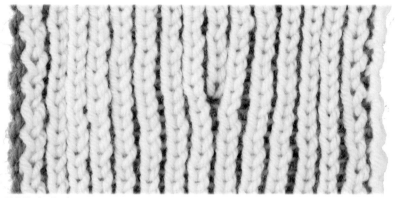

Rolled Edge ◄ | ► Knit Under Purl

GARTER STITCH

Alternating colors as established and holding the yarns ready for the Twigg-stitch row, knit the first two stitches and knit the last two stitches of every row. This method is a simple way to create decorative edges.

For a stronger alternative, knit these stitches with both yarns held together.

ROLLED EDGE

Alternating colors as established and holding the yarns ready for the Twigg-stitch row, purl the first two stitches and knit the last two stitches of every row. Do not twist the yarns around each other at the beginning of the row and be sure to tighten the yarns a bit after the first two stitches to maintain even tension. This method forms very tidy rolled edges.

KNIT UNDER PURL

At the beginning of every row, bring the knit yarn under the purl yarn (**Photo 1**) to extend the twists to the selvedge. This method can form somewhat untidy edges, but it's ideal if you plan to pick up stitches from these edges or sew them into seams.

Color-Switch Patterns

Twigg stitch offers the unique opportunity to create colorwork patterns by simply switching how the yarns are held so that the knit-color yarn is purled and the purl-color yarn is knitted. The key to a balanced fabric lies in how the yarns are switched in your hands. Color switch is always worked over an even number of stitches and always begins with a knit stitch so that the pattern is mirrored on the two sides of the fabric.

There are two ways to switch the yarns for these patterns. One method produces an extra twist between the two yarns, the other takes out the twist. For a balanced fabric and to prevent the yarns from becoming irretrievably tangled, you'll need to alternate between the two methods.

You can add an extra twist at the beginning of the pattern stitches, then omit the twist when returning to the original background color assignments, or you can omit the twist at the beginning of the pattern stitches, then add an extra twist when returning to the original colors. How you choose to work only matters when the color changes are stacked one above another on successive rows. One method will cause the stitches to sit a little farther apart; the other will cause them to sit just a little closer together. When stacked vertically on consecutive rows, both methods can produce a noticeable unevenness in the rib. To prevent this, alternate the way you change the yarns so that a color change involving no twist is positioned directly above a color change that introduced an extra twist, and vice versa. This often happens naturally when you're knitting flat in rows, but you'll want to pay attention to maintain this alternation when working in rounds.

Adding an Extra Twist

HOLDING BOTH YARNS IN THE SAME HAND: Begin with the yarn held for the color section just finished (**Photo 1**). Bring the knit yarn forward to the left of the purl yarn to make an extra twist (**Photo 2**) and into the purl position while letting the purl yarn move into the knit position.

HOLDING ONE YARN IN EACH HAND: Begin with the yarn held for the color section just finished (**Photo 3**). Bring the knit yarn forward and in front of the purl yarn (**Photo 4**).

BOTH METHODS: To keep track of the amount of twist, always keep hold of at least one yarn as you switch the colors. Readjust the yarns so that they feel balanced before you continue knitting.

Taking Out the Extra Twist

HOLDING BOTH YARNS IN THE SAME HAND: Begin with the yarn held for the color section just finished (**Photo 5**). Bring the knit yarn forward to the right of the purl yarn and into the purl position while letting the purl yarn move back into the knit position (**Photo 6**).

HOLDING ONE YARN IN EACH HAND: Begin with the yarn held for the color section just finished (**Photo 7**). Bring the purl yarn forward and in front of the knit yarn (**Photo 8**).

BOTH METHODS: To keep track of the amount of twist, always keep hold of at least one yarn as you switch the colors. Readjust the yarns so that they feel balanced before you continue knitting.

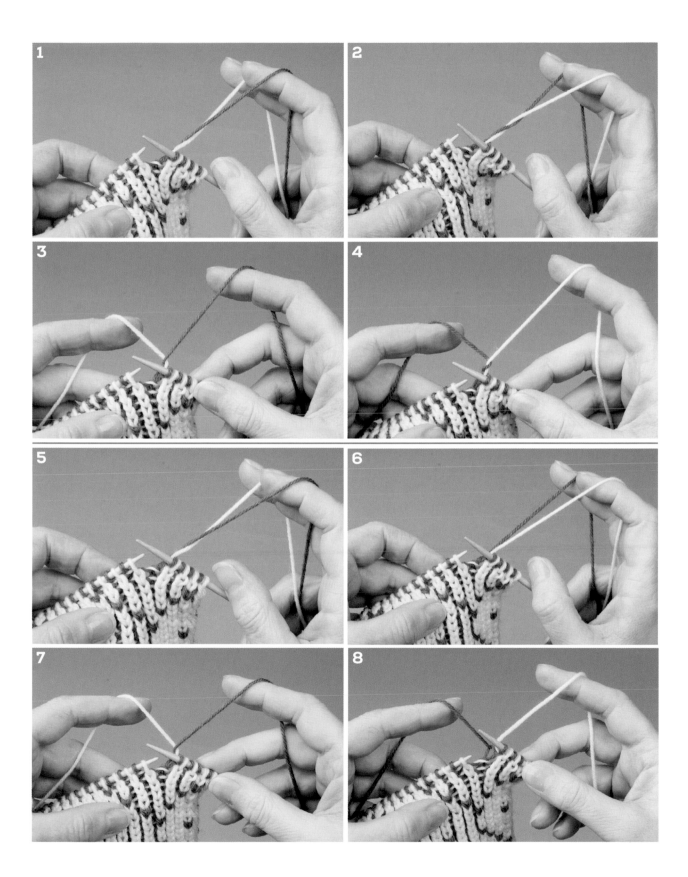

Picking Up Stitches

If you plan to pick up stitches along a selvedge, you'll want to begin with a selvedge in which the knit yarn was brought under the purl yarn at the beginning of every row so that both yarns extend to the edge.

Hold the knitting so that the bind-off edge is to your right and so that you're looking at the backs of the edge stitches. Notice that there is a series of bars between the first and second stitches where the two yarns twist around each other.

Working from left to right, insert the knitting needle into the first double-yarn where you see the knit color twist on top of the purl color (**Photo 1**), skip the next double bar, insert the needle into the third double bar (**Photo 2**), and continue lifting alternate double bars along the selvedge (**Photo 3**). In the sample shown, 12 double bars have been picked up from 24 rows of knitting. Each double bar on the needle represents two stitches. (Pick up a stitch in the cast-on or bind-off edge if you need an extra pick-up point.)

To work the first row, make a slipknot of the two working yarns and place it on a spare needle. Hold the knit yarn in the purl position and the purl yarn in the knit position to work in double knitting (**Photo 4**). Work into each double bar two times, first knit it with the knit yarn (**Photo 5**), then purl it with the purl yarn (**Photo 6**) to form one stitch for each row of knitting (**Photos 7 and 8**), being careful not to twist the yarns between the stitches. Change to regular Twigg stitch for the second row.

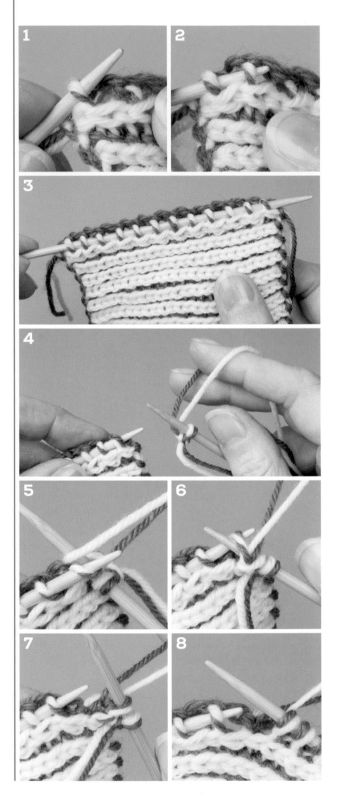

Working in Rounds

The only difference when working in rounds, rather than back and forth in rows, is that the same side of the fabric always faces you, so you can hold the colors the same way throughout.

If you have trouble joining without twisting the cast-on stitches, work one row before joining to help ensure that the stitches are straight (you can eliminate the short split when you weave in the ends). However, doing so also means you'll want to plan the order of the knit and purl stitches on your cast-on so that they will appear the way you want them on the first round. For example, if you use one of the long-tail variations for casting on, you'll want to make sure the first stitch cast on is in your chosen knit color.

If you use double-pointed needles, take care to maintain the proper yarn twists between the stitches at the needle boundaries.

Determining Gauge and Taking Measurements

It's always important to knit a gauge swatch before you embark on a full project, especially if you want it to fit. Not only will this swatch tell you the number of stitches and rows per inch of Twigg stitch, it will also give you a chance to evaluate whether or not you like the feel of the fabric produced by the yarn and needles you've chosen.

In general, you should knit a Twigg-stitch swatch that's at least a 4" (10 cm) square, and you should wash and block that swatch to determine how it behaves. Some yarns, particularly those made from natural fibers, will spread out a bit with blocking, resulting in a different gauge. Be sure to measure your gauge before and after blocking, so there won't be any surprises.

Keep in mind that, like any ribbed pattern, Twigg stitch is quite stretchy. This characteristic makes measuring gauge more challenging than with regular stockinette stitch. Don't pull on the fabric widthwise when you measure the stitch or row gauge. In general, you'll get a more accurate gauge measurement if you rely on the number of rows per inch instead of the number of stitches per inch because there isn't as much lengthwise stretch.

I find that my gauge is affected by the way I tension the yarn. My knitting looks the best when I hold both yarns in my right hand, probably because I'm a lifelong English knitter. Try the different methods described on pages 11 to 13 to determine what works best for you.

Although most types of knitting produce stitches that are slightly wider than they are tall (resulting in more rows than stitches per inch), Twigg stitches tend to be nearly square and to relax widthwise with use. This squareness makes it much easier to pick up stitches along selvedges—simply pick up one stitch for every row.

Keep in mind that because Twigg-stitch fabrics have considerable widthwise stretch, it's best to count rows instead of measure inches (centimeters) while a project is on the needles. Provided you took accurate gauge measurements, doing so will ensure that all lengthwise measurements will be consistent.

Weaving In Ends

I like to weave in the ends "invisibly" by following the path of several knitted stitches, using a sharp-point needle to pierce the same color of yarn I'm following for a few stitches. I like to use chenille needles that have eyes large enough to accommodate the yarn and points sharp enough to pierce the yarn. This method ensures that the yarn ends are secure and that the knitting remains stretchy.

Correcting Mistakes

You're bound to make some mistakes when working Twigg stitch, especially in the beginning. Some mistakes can be remedied while the stitches are on the needles, others can't. I've described the most common mistakes below and how to fix them.

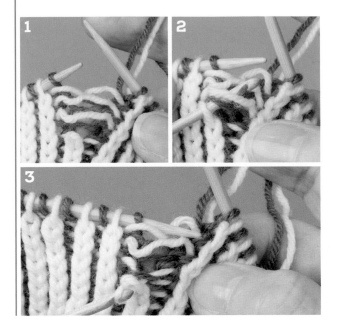

DROPPED STITCH

A dropped stitch will leave a column of double horizontal strands (one of each color) as it progresses down the knitting. The strand that formed the stitch will be a bit longer than the strand that simply traversed across that stitch (**Photo 1**). To pick up the dropped stitch, use a crochet hook to "ladder up" the dropped stitch to the needles, making sure to grab the longer loop for each row from under the shorter one (**Photo 2**) and then pulling this loop through the live stitch (**Photo 3**).

ACCIDENTAL YARNOVER

If you find that one of the yarns forms an unwanted yarnover on the needle (**Photo 1**), simply drop it off the needle toward the purl side of the stitch (**Photo 2**).

PURL BAR SHOWING IN FRONT OF A KNIT STITCH

It's not uncommon to create a bar of the purl yarn across the front of a knit stitch (**Photo 1**). To correct it, drop the knit stitch to one stitch below the bar (**Photo 2**), then use a crochet hook to pick up the stitch as described above. If you need to drop down several rows, you can hold the knit loops on a knitting or cable needle (**Photo 3**) to help maintain the established color pattern.

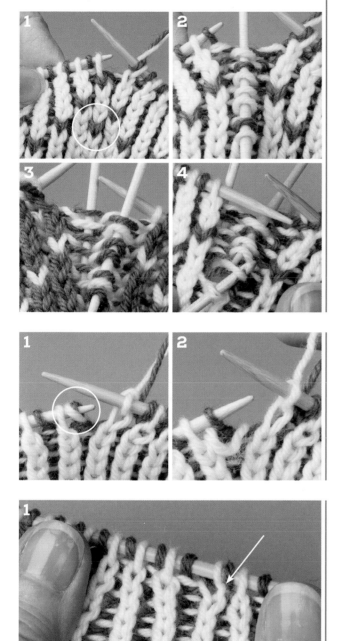

STITCHES WORKED IN THE WRONG COLORS

If you inadvertently work a pair of stitches in the wrong colors (Twigg-knit with the purl yarn and Twigg-purl with the knit yarn; **Photo 1**), simply let both stitches drop down to the row below the mistake. Hold the dropped loops on a cable or knitting needle, using separate needles for the "right" (**Photo 2**) and "wrong" sides (**Photo 3**). Working each side separately, use a crochet hook to pick up the stitches in the correct color (**Photo 4**).

If you worked just one stitch in the wrong color, there won't be enough yarn of the other color to fix the error. In this case, you'll have to rip out to the miscolored stitch and continue with the correct colors.

STITCH WORKED WITH BOTH YARNS TOGETHER

If you find that you've accidentally worked a stitch while holding both yarns together (**Photo 1**), first try dropping the extra strand (in this case, white) to the front for a purl stitch (**Photo 2**) or to the back for a knit stitch. Depending on the yarn, the extra length may be absorbed by the neighboring stitches to completely hide the mistake. If the extra yarn remains visible, you'll have to rip out to correct the error.

NO TWIST BETWEEN ADJACENT STITCHES

Failure to twist the two yarns between adjacent stitches may cause the ribs to pull together (**Photo 1**). Depending on the yarn, this may be subtle or quite noticeable. If you don't like the look, you'll have to rip back to correct the error—there's no way to drop down and create a twist that isn't there.

3 THE PROJECTS

The ten projects that follow are designed to give you a solid foundation for working Twigg stitch. For the most straightforward start, begin with the **Collegiate Scarf** (page 50), which will be forgiving if you don't match the gauge exactly. Knitted in basic Twigg stitch, this scarf features a different eye-catching stripe pattern on each side. As your confidence builds, try one of the other projects to learn how different Twigg-stitch techniques are applied.

For a completely different sort of look, the textured effect in the **Lake Shore Wrap** (page 54) results from a combination of horizontal and vertical stripes worked in Twigg-stitch seed stitch. The striking play of colors is reminiscent of woven cloth. When you're ready to add a bit of shaping, try the **Buttoned Hat & Fingerless Mitts** (page 70), both of which are knitted back and forth in rows and joined with buttons for completely reversible wear.

To demonstrate how easy it is to work Twigg-stitch in rounds, I've included an infinity scarf and three hats, all of which employ the signature color-switch technique. A Möbius cast-on is fundamental to the shape and dark-on-light and light-on-dark color pattern in the **Möbius Infinity Scarf** (page 58). The more challenging **Brooke Beret** (page 64) is worked from the top down and shaped with increases to reveal wide panels of cables outlined with simple color-switch stitches. Also worked from the top down, the graphic pattern in **Double Diamond Beanie** (page 98) illustrates how a simple color-switch design can make a bold statement. The **Snowflake Earflap Hat** (page 104) is worked from the bottom up, beginning with short-row shaping for the earflaps. The two colors in the hat are combined in colorful braided ties.

Many of my favorite designs are developed from "building-block" elements that are repeated or extended. The diamond-shaped units that make up the **Fan Shawl** (page 78) build upon one another to form gently curving edges that stay put around the shoulders. The two lacy "wings" of the **Mothwing Scarf** (page 90) are formed from interlocking diamond motifs that grow outward from a narrow center. It drapes beautifully and is a delight to wear.

As a collection, these projects represent the techniques outlined in Chapter 2 (page 10), including various ways to cast on, bind off, decrease, increase, and work selvedge stitches. For many of the projects, though, the specific technique can be a matter of personal choice; feel free to substitute other options to suit your preferences. For example, you might want to use a more decorative or simpler cast-on or bind-off than I've chosen. Or, you might want to use more or fewer colors or substitute one of the stitch patterns provided in the stitch dictionary in Chapter 4 (page 110). Once you're familiar with the basics of Twigg stitch, these adjustments will be as straightforward as in regular knitting, and you'll be able to use the patterns as a foundation for branching out into your own experiments and creativity.

Collegiate
SCARF

This scarf is a very good introduction to Twigg stitch. It's worked with three colors of yarns that switch position between Twigg-knit and Twigg-purl stitches. On one face, twenty-row stripes of green alternate with two-row stripes of yellow or purple; on the other face, each twenty-row stripe of yellow or purple is split in the middle by a two-row stripe of green. The look of the single-color ribbed-cable cast-on at one end is matched by Vicki's single-color ribbed-chain bind-off at the other. The first two stitches of every row are slipped for tidy selvedges. Use the colors shown here or make substitutions for a scarf that's uniquely yours.

FINISHED SIZE
About 6" (15 cm) wide and 55" (139.5 cm) long.

Yarn
Fingering weight (#1 Super Fine).

Shown here: Shibui Staccato (70% superwash merino, 30% silk; 191 yd [175 m]/50 g): Lime (green; A), 2 skeins; Velvet (purple; B) and Brass (yellow; C), 1 skein each.

Needles
Size U.S. 3 (3.25 mm): straight or circular.

Adjust needle size if necessary to obtain the correct gauge.

Notions
Sharp-point tapestry needle.

Gauge
40 sts and 32 rows = 4" (10 cm) in Twigg stitch.

Techniques

Stitch Guide

Tk: Twigg-knit so that the knit yarn traps the purl yarn.

Tp: Twigg-purl so that the purl yarn traps the knit yarn.

NOTES

To make a tidy cast-on corner and to smooth color transitions between stripes, do not slip the first two stitches for the selvedge the first time Row 1 is worked in each pattern repeat. Instead, begin the first row of the stripe by working these two stitches as Tk1 with B (or C), Tp1 with A. ● To make a tidy transition between the B and C stripes and keep the colors of the slipped edge stitches consistent throughout, the last two stitches of Row 22 are slipped in the same way as before.

Scarf

With A, use the single-color ribbed-cable method (see page 15) to CO 60 sts.

Join B by tying it around the cast-on row a couple of sts away from the edge.

ROW 1: (knit with B; purl with A) Sl 2 using the slip-stitch selvedge technique (except for the first row of each stripe of B or C; see Notes), *Tk1 (see Stitch Guide), Tp1 (see Stitch Guide); rep from *.

ROW 2: (knit with A; purl with B) Sl 2, *Tk1, Tp1; rep from *.

ROWS 3–10: Rep Rows 1 and 2 four more times, slipping the first 2 sts of each row.

ROW 11: (knit with A; purl with B) Sl 2, *Tk1, Tp1; rep from * to last 2 sts, switch the position of the two yarns by taking B to the right of A to twist the yarns an extra time, Tk1 with B, Tp1 with A so the edge sts are always the same colors.

ROW 12: (knit with B; purl with A) Sl 2, *Tk1, Tp1; rep from * to last 2 sts, switch the yarns as on Row 11, Tk1 with A, Tp1 with B.

ROWS 13–22: Rep Rows 1 and 2 five times, slipping the first 2 sts of each row and ending 2 sts before the end of Row 22, sl 2 (see Notes).

Cut B and join C by tying the tails together to secure.

ROWS 23–44: Using C instead of B, work as for Rows 1–22, beg at * in Row 1.

Cut C and rejoin B by tying the tails together to secure.

Rep Rows 1–44 nine more times, ending Row 44 of the last rep by working in established patt to the end of the row (do not slip the last 2 sts)—440 rows total; piece measures about 55" (139.5 cm) from CO. Cut C.

NEXT ROW: With A, *k1, p1; rep from * to end.

Starting with ssk, use Vicki's single-color ribbed method (see page 26) to BO all sts.

Finishing

Remove knot attaching B to the CO edge.

Weave in loose ends separately and as invisibly as possible (see page 45).

Lake Shore
WRAP

The woven-plaid look of this rectangular wrap is achieved with a simple seed-stitch pattern combined with vertical intarsia columns and horizontal stripes to create a subtle interplay of colors. The wrap begins with blocks of single-color ribbed-cable cast-on and ends with matching blocks of Vicki's single-color ribbed bind-off. Twigg seed stitch is worked similarly to regular seed stitch by knitting the purl stitches and purling the knit stitches as they appear. It takes a bit of attention to maintain this alternation, but the results are well worth the effort.

FINISHED SIZE
About 15" (38 cm) wide and 60" (152.5 cm) long.

Yarn
Sportweight (#2 Fine).

Shown here: Malabrigo Arroyo (100% superwash merino; 335 yd [306 m]/100 g): #46 Prussian Blue (blue; A), #48 Glitter (gold; B), #45 Chircas (olive; C), and #855 Aguas (light teal; D), 1 skein each.

Needles
Size U.S. 6 (4 mm): straight.

Adjust needle size if necessary to obtain the correct gauge.

Notions
Removable markers; sharp-point tapestry needle.

Gauge
28 sts and 23½ rows = 4" (10 cm) in Twigg seed stitch from Rows 1 and 2 of instructions.

Techniques

○ Single-color ribbed-cable cast-on, page 15.

○ Vicki's single-color ribbed bind-off, page 26.

Stitch Guide

Tk: Twigg-knit so that the knit yarn traps the purl yarn.

Tp: Twigg-purl so that the purl yarn traps the knit yarn.

Tp2tog: Twigg-purl 2 stitches together (1 of each color) using the purl yarn.

NOTES

Divide each skein in half and designate one half for the vertical (lengthwise) columns and the other half for the horizontal (widthwise) stripes. ● Yarns are referred to as A (blue), B (gold), C (olive), and D (teal), ranging from darkest to lightest. The two halves of each skein are numbered, so A1, B1, C1, and D1 indicate the half-skeins used for the vertical intarsia columns, and A2, B2, C2, and D2 indicate the half-skeins used for the horizontal stripes. ● To distinguish the yarns used for the vertical columns from the yarns used for the horizontal stripes, place a removable marker around the working strand of yarns A2, B2, C2, and D2. Let these markers slide down each yarn as you work. ● When working the vertical intarsia columns, the first stitch of each new color will be a knit stitch on the odd-numbered rows and will be a purl stitch on the even-numbered rows. ● To change the yarn color on a knit stitch, place the old color on top of the new color at the back of the work, then pick up the new color from under the old to twist the two yarns. ● To change the yarn color on a purl stitch, drop the old color in the front, then pick up the new color from beside it so that the two colors do not twist. ● For neat edges, bring the yarn for the first stitch (horizontal stripe yarn) under the yarn for the second stitch (vertical column yarn) at the beginning of every row.

Wrap

After dividing each skein in half (see Notes), make a slipknot of A1 and place it on the left needle tip to anchor the yarn; the slipknot does not count as a st and will be dropped later.

> **note:** The nature of the cable cast-on is that when you change colors the new yarn comes through and wraps under the last stitch of the old color on the needle. Therefore, the stitches are deliberately not cast-on in four groups of 26 stitches, but the colors in the cast-on edge will appear to align with the four 26-stitch columns in the final result.

CO 105 sts as foll:

STEP 1: With A1, use the e-wrap method (see page 14) to CO 1 st next to the slipknot, then use the ribbed-cable method (see page 15) to [CO 1 st knitwise, CO 1 st purlwise] 13 times, CO 1 st knitwise, then drop A1—28 A1 sts (not counting the slipknot).

STEP 2: Cont with B1 to [CO 1 st purlwise, CO 1 st knitwise] 13 times, then drop B1—26 B1 sts.

STEP 3: Cont with C1, CO 26 sts as in Step 2, then drop C1—26 C1 sts.

STEP 4: Cont with D1 to [CO 1 st purlwise, CO 1 st knitwise] 12 times, CO 1 st purlwise. To make a tidy corner, knit the last CO st, tighten the yarn a little at the base

ROW 2: Using A2 for all knit sts, [Tp1 with A1, Tk1] 13 times, change to B1 for purl sts (see Notes), [Tp1 with B1, Tk1] 13 times, change to C1 for purl sts, [Tp1 with C1, Tk1] 13 times, change to D1 for purl sts, [Tp1 with D1, Tk1] 13 times.

ROWS 3–22: Rep Rows 1 and 2 ten more times.

Cut A2 and join B2 by tying their tails together to secure. Place a removable marker around the working strand of B2.

ROW 23: Using B2 for all purl sts, rep Row 1.

ROW 24: Using B2 for all knit sts, rep Row 2.

ROWS 25–44: Rep Rows 23 and 24 ten more times.

Cut B2 and join C2 by tying their tails together to secure. Place a removable marker around the working strand of C2.

ROW 45: Using C2 for all purl sts, rep Row 1.

ROW 46: Using C2 for all knit sts, rep Row 2.

ROWS 47–66: Rep Rows 45 and 46 ten more times.

Cut C2 and join D2 by tying their tails together to secure. Place a removable marker around the working strand of D2.

ROW 67: Using D2 for all purl sts, rep Row 1.

ROW 68: Using D2 for all knit sts, rep Row 2.

ROWS 69–88: Rep Rows 67 and 68 ten more times.

Cut D2 and join A2 by tying their tails together to secure. Place a removable marker around the working strand of A2.

Rep Rows 1–88 three more times—352 rows total; piece measures about 60" (152.5 cm) from CO. Cut D2.

With the odd-numbered-row side of the piece facing and beginning with ssk, use Vicki's single-color ribbed method (see page 26) to BO 26 sts with D1, then BO 26 sts with C1, then BO 26 sts with B1, then BO the rem 26 sts with A1.

Finishing

Weave in all loose ends separately and as invisibly as possible (see page 45).

of this knit st, then place the new corner st on the left needle tip—25 D1 sts; 105 sts total (excluding slipknot).

Join A2 by tying it to the CO edge a few sts in from the edge to anchor the yarns for Twigg stitch. To help distinguish A1 and A2, place a removable marker around the working strand of A2 (see Notes). If desired, place a marker after every 26 sts in the first row to mark where the colors change.

ROW 1: Using A2 for all purl sts, [Tk1 with D1, Tp1] 13 times, change to C1 for knit sts (see Notes), [Tk1 with C1, Tp1] 13 times, change to B1 for knit sts, [Tk1 with B1, Tp1] 13 times, change to A1 for knit sts, [Tk1 with A1, Tp1] 13 times, working last st as Tp2tog (see Stitch Guide) instead of Tp1 on the very first row to make a good corner and to dec the extra st, then drop the slipknot—104 sts.

Möbius
INFINITY SCARF

The Möbius shape is a perfect place to show off a color-switch design. The colors in the simple pattern are automatically reversed as each half of the scarf grows outward from the two-color Möbius cast-on. This means that you'll work every round of the chart with the same side facing you. The knit and purl yarns exchange roles to create what looks like a color-stranded design, but without the stranding. The edges are finished with a subtle lace pattern followed by your choice of a single-color or a two-color ribbed bind-off.

FINISHED SIZE
About 48" (122 cm) in circumference and 9" (23 cm) wide.

Yarn
Fingering weight (#1 Super Fine).

Shown here: Malabrigo Sock (100% superwash merino; 440 yd [402 m]/100 g): #63 Natural (A), #138 Ivy (variegated grass green; B), and #863 Zarzamora (variegated lavender and aqua; C), 1 skein each.

Note: Each scarf will use about 350 yd (320 m) of A and 175 yd (160 m) each of B and C.

Needles
Size U.S. 4 (3.5 mm): 40" (100 cm) or longer circular (cir).

Adjust needle size if necessary to obtain the correct gauge.

Notions
19 markers (m; 1 in a unique color or style to mark the end of the rnd); sharp-point tapestry needle.

Note: Use thin stitch markers that won't distort the spaces between the stitches.

Gauge
35 sts and 32 rnds = 4" (10 cm) in Twigg stitch, worked in rnds.

Techniques

- ◯ Basic Twigg stitch, page 10.
- ◯ Möbius cast-on, page 24.
- ◯ Twigg stitch color-switch, page 42.
- ◯ Vicki's two-color ribbed bind-off, page 30 or Vicki's single-color rib bind-off, page 26.

Stitch Guide

Tk: Twigg-knit so that the knit yarn traps the purl yarn.

Tp: Twigg-purl so that the purl yarn traps the knit yarn.

Tk3tog: Twigg-knit 3 stitches together (2 knit stitches plus the purl stitch between them) using the knit yarn.

Tp3tog: Twigg-purl 3 stitches together (2 purl stitches plus the knit stitch between them) using the purl yarn.

ryo: (reverse yarnover) Bring both yarns from back to front over the top of the right needle tip and between the two needles to the back again to create a double-strand loop with a reverse mount. On the following row, work Tk1, Tp1 into the back of the double-strand loop—2 sts made from 2-strand ryo (see page 37).

CHANGING COLORS IN TWIGG STITCH COLOR-SWITCH

The color-switch pattern for the Möbius Infinity Scarf has a background worked with A for the Twigg-knit stitches and B or C for the Twigg-purl stitches. To create the pattern, temporarily exchange the colors so that B or C is used for the knit stitches and A is used for the purl stitches. After working the pattern stitches, switch the colors back to their original assignments: knit with A, purl with B or C. To keep the fabric balanced, handle the yarns at the color changes as follows:

ODD-NUMBERED ROUNDS

Switch B or C to knit and A to purl: Exchange the position of the two yarns in your hand(s), adding an extra twist, then work the marked sts (always an even number) using B or C to knit and A to purl, maintaining the rib as established.

To switch the colors back to original positions: Exchange the two yarns the other way to take out the twist, then continue with the original colors.

EVEN-NUMBERED ROUNDS

Switch B or C to knit and A to purl: Exchange the position of the two yarns in your hand(s) to take out the twist, then work the marked sts (always an even number) using B or C to knit and A to purl, maintaining the rib as established.

To switch the colors back to original positions: Exchange the two yarns the other way to add an extra twist, then continue with the original colors.

NOTES

Do not cut yarns B and C between stripes. Instead, carry the unused color up along the junction between the beginning and end of the round until it's needed again. At the start of each round, bring the carried yarn up vertically, threading it between the two working yarns, then dropping it to the back of the work. Be careful not to pull the carried yarn too tight, or it will cause the fabric to pucker. ● To begin working with the carried color again, simply drop the old color to the back and begin working with the new color, making sure it isn't pulled too tightly. At the start of the following round, bring the unused color up between the two current working yarns as before.

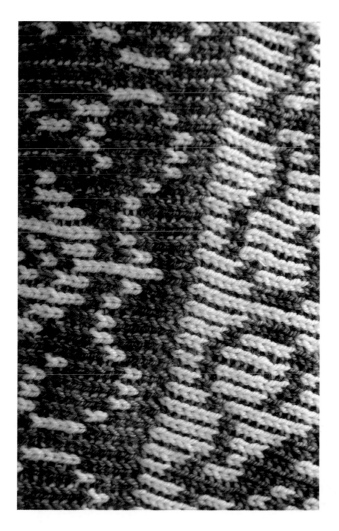

Scarf

With A and B held together, make a slipknot and place it on the left needle tip. Slide the left needle to the right so that the slipknot sits on the cable behind the needle. Hold A for the knit sts over your index finger and B for the purl sts over your thumb, and being careful not to let go with your left hand until all the sts have been CO, use the Möbius method (see page 24) to CO 418 sts as foll: [CO 44 sts, place marker (pm)] 9 times, then CO 22 more sts—9 marked groups of 44 sts plus 22 sts. To end, bring the two yarns down and to the front, wrap them up over the cable, then under the right needle tip to the back in position to knit.

Spread the sts out around the double-cable loop so that the slipknot arrives on the left needle tip—the cable will cross over once, the CO sts will be on the cable under the left needle, and the double-yarn sts (one strand of each color) of the "hem" will be on the left needle.

> **note:** The double-yarn stitches will alternate between being mounted properly on the needle (with the leading leg in the front) and mounted in the reverse orientation on the needle (with the leading leg in the back); the mount will be corrected as you continue with the set up.

Drop the slipknot from the needle but don't undo it. Tension the two yarns for Twigg st so that A will be used for the knit sts and B will be used for the purl sts.

SET-UP RND: (knit with A; purl with B) *Tk1 into the back of the first double-yarn st to correct the mount, Tp1 into next double-yarn st; rep from *, placing a marker after the first 22 sts, then after every 44 sts, ending with the unique marker at the dropped slipknot—836 sts total in 19 marked 44-st sections. Because you're working on both the top and bottom edges of the knitting, each complete round will contain double the number of sts CO.

Work patt from Möbius Floral chart (see page 63) as foll:

RNDS 1 AND 2: (knit with A; purl with B) *Tk1, Tp1; rep from * to end-of-rnd m, slipping markers (sl m) as you come to them.

RND 3: Exchanging colors for odd-numbered rnds as described on page 60, *work 10 sts as established, 2 sts in

color-switch (knit with B; purl with A), 10 sts as established, 6 sts in color-switch, 10 sts as established, 6 sts in color switch; rep from *.

Do not cut B. Tie C to B close to needles and drop B to the back.

RND 4: Work as for Rnd 3, substituting C for B and exchanging colors for even-numbered rnds as described on page 60.

RNDS 5–24: Carrying the unused color up to where it is needed again (see Notes) and exchanging yarns for color-switches as established, work Rnds 5–24 of chart—piece measures about 3" (7.5 cm) on each side of CO.

> note: The last two rounds, which complete the flower motifs, are worked as transition Rnds 25 and 26 and are not shown on the chart.

Edging

Slipping the established markers as you come to them, work 2 transition rnds between charts as foll:

RND 25: With A and B, *work 10 sts as established, 2 sts in color-switch, 10 sts as established, ryo (see Stitch Guide) with both yarns held tog, 22 sts as established, ryo; rep from *—912 sts total, counting each ryo as 2 sts; each 44-st section has inc'd to 48 sts.

RND 26: With A and B, *work 10 sts as established, 2 sts in color-switch, 10 sts as established, [Tk1, Tp1] into double strand of ryo, 22 sts as established, [Tk1, Tp1] into ryo; rep from *.

Cont in patt from Möbius Lace chart as foll:

RND 27: (knit with A; purl with B) *Tk1, Tp3tog (see Stitch Guide) with B, [Tk1, Tp1] 7 times, Tk3tog (see Stitch Guide) with A, Tp1, ryo, work 2 sts as established, ryo; rep from *.

RND 28: (knit with A; purl with C) Work as established, working [Tk1, Tp1] into every ryo.

RNDS 29–36: Knitting with A and purling with B or C as shown, work in patt to end of chart, working [Tk1, Tp1] in each ryo as before—edging measures about 1½" (3.8 cm); piece measures about 4½" (11.5 cm) on each side of CO.

MÖBIUS FLORAL

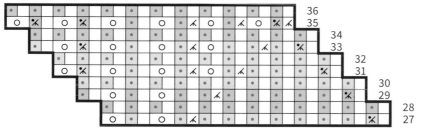

44-st repeat
See instructions for Rnds 25 and 26.

MÖBIUS LACE

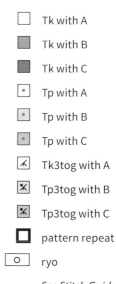

24-st repeat

	Tk with A
	Tk with B
	Tk with C
	Tp with A
	Tp with B
	Tp with C
	Tk3tog with A
	Tp3tog with B
	Tp3tog with C
	pattern repeat
	ryo

*See Stitch Guide
for abbreviations.*

With A in the knit position and C in the purl position,
use Vicki's two-color ribbed method (see page 30) or,
with your choice of color, use Vicki's single-color ribbed
method (see page 26) to BO all sts.

Finishing

Weave in loose ends separately and as invisibly as possible (see page 45).

Brooke BERET

This beret-style slouch hat features wide cables outlined by single columns of color-switch Twigg stitches. The hat begins with a circular cast-on at the top of the crown, after which stitches are increased to the full diameter, then decreased on smaller needles for the band. It's finished with Vicki's single-color ribbed bind-off worked to fit the k2, p2 ribbing of the band.

FINISHED SIZE

About 20½" (52 cm) unstretched band circumference, 30" (76 cm) circumference at widest part (Rnds 31–46 of chart), and 7½" (19 cm) long from CO to start of band.

Yarn

DK weight (#3 Light).

Shown here: Malabrigo Silky Merino (50% silk, 50% baby merino; 150 yd [137 m]/50 g): #850 Archangel (rose; A) and #856 Azules (blue; B), 1 skein each.

Note: One hat requires about 121 yd (111 m) of each color.

Needles

Hat body: size U.S. 6 (4 mm): set of 5 double-pointed (dpn).

Band: size U.S. 3 (3.25 mm): set of 5 dpn.

Adjust needle size if necessary to obtain the correct gauge.

Notions

Marker (m); cable needle (cn); sharp-point tapestry needle.

Gauge

34 sts and 24½ rnds = 4" (10 cm) in Twigg stitch, worked in rnds on larger needles.

Techniques

○ Basic Twigg stitch, page 10.

○ Branched increase, page 39.

○ Twigg-stitch color-switch, page 42.

○ Vicki's single-color ribbed bind-off for k2, p2 ribbing, page 26.

Stitch Guide

Tk: Twigg-knit so that the knit yarn traps the purl yarn.

Tp: Twigg-purl so that the purl yarn traps the knit yarn.

Tk2tog: Twigg-knit 2 stitches together (1 of each color) using the knit yarn.

Tp2tog: Twigg-purl 2 stitches together (1 of each color) using the purl yarn.

ryo: (reverse yarnover) Bring both yarns from back to front over the top of the right needle tip and between the two needles to the back again to create a double-strand loop with a reverse mount.

On the following row, work Tk1, Tp1 into the back of the double-strand loop—2 sts made from 2-strand ryo (see page 37).

4/4LC: Slip 4 sts onto cable needle and hold in front of work, work 4 sts in established Twigg-stitch patt, then work the 4 sts from the cable needle in the established Twigg-stitch patt.

4/4RC: Slip 4 sts onto cable needle and hold in back of work, work 4 sts in established Twigg-stitch patt, then work the 4 sts from the cable needle in the established Twigg-stitch patt.

WORKING THE COLOR-SWITCH OUTLINE STITCHES

This hat is worked predominantly with color A facing with single Twigg-stitch columns of color B outlining the cables. To create the outlines, the colors are temporarily exchanged so that B is used for the knit stitches and A is used for the purl stitches. After working the outline stitches, the colors switch back to their original positions. To keep the fabric balanced, handle the yarns at the color changes as follows:

ODD-NUMBERED ROUNDS
Switch B to knit and A to purl: Exchange the position of the two yarns in your hand(s), adding an extra twist, then work the 2 outline stitches using B to knit and A to purl, maintaining the rib as established.

To switch the colors back to original positions: Exchange the two yarns the other way to take out the twist, then continue with the original colors.

EVEN-NUMBERED ROUNDS
Switch B to knit and A to purl: Exchange the position of the two yarns in your hand(s) to take out the twist, then work the 2 outline stitches using B to knit and A to purl, maintaining the rib as established.

To switch the colors back to original positions: Exchange the two yarns the other way to add an extra twist, then continue with the original colors.

Beret

With larger needles and holding both yarns tog, make a slipknot and place it on a needle held in your left hand, then use the e-wrap method (see page 14) to make a loop with both yarns next to the slipknot. Without removing the e-wrap loop from the needle and using A for the knit sts and B for the purl sts, *work [Tk1, Tp1] 4 times into the e-wrap loop; use another needle to rep from *, then slip the e-wrap loop from the left needle—16 sts total; 8 sts on each needle. Drop the slipknot from the needle. Do not turn work.

Shape Crown

note: Throughout the crown shaping, knit with A and purl with B, except when color-switch (knit with B; purl with A) is specified.

Work in rnds as foll:

RND 1: *Tk1, Tp1; rep from *.

RND 2: Place marker (pm) for beg of rnd, *use the branched increase method (see page 39) to [increase the next 2-st rib to 4 sts] 2 times; rep from *, beginning a new needle after every 8 sts—32 sts total; 8 sts each on 4 needles.

RND 3: *Work 4 sts as established, ryo (see Stitch Guide), work 4 sts as established; rep from * 3 more times.

RND 4: *Work 4 sts as established, work [Tk1, Tp1] 2 times in ryo, work 4 sts as established; rep from *—48 sts; 12 sts each needle.

RND 5: *Work 6 sts as established, ryo, work 6 sts as established; rep from *.

RND 6: *Work 6 sts as established, work [Tk1, Tp1] 2 times in ryo, work 6 sts as established; rep from *—64 sts; 16 sts each needle.

Remove beg-of-rnd marker, work 8 sts as established, replace m for new beg of rnd—rnd now begins after first 8 sts of first dpn. Rearrange sts between needles as necessary to work the cables.

RND 7: *Ryo, work 4 sts as established, 4/4RC (see Stitch Guide), work 4 sts as established; rep from *.

RND 8: Switching colors as described on page 66 for even-numbered rnds, *work [Tk1 with B, Tp1 with A] 2 times in ryo, change colors back to original positions,

work 16 sts as established; rep from *—80 sts; 20 sts each needle.

RND 9: Switching colors as described on page 66 for odd-numbered rnds, *work 2 sts in color-switch, ryo, work 2 sts in color-switch, switch colors back and work 16 sts in original colors.

note: Continue to exchange yarns for color-switch stitches in this way on all following rounds.

RND 10: *Work 2 sts in color-switch, work [Tk1, Tp1] 2 times in ryo with original colors, work 2 sts in color-switch, work 16 sts in original colors; rep from *—96 sts; 24 sts each needle.

RND 11: *Work 2 sts in color-switch, switch back to original colors, ryo, [Tk1, Tp1] 2 times, ryo, work 2 sts in color-switch, work 4/4LC 2 times in original colors; rep from *.

RND 12: *Work 2 sts in color-switch, with original colors work [Tk1, Tp1] 4 times working 2 sts in each ryo, work

CABLE

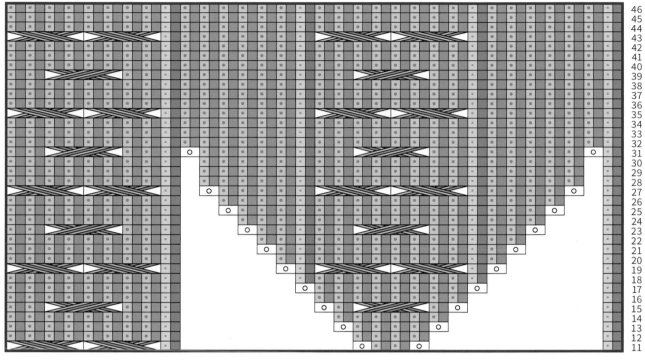

46
45
44
43
42
41
40
39
38
37
36
35
34
33
32
31
30
29
28
27
26
25
24
23
22
21
20
19
18
17
16
15
14
13
12
11

24-st repeat
inc'd to 64-st repeat

2 sts in color-switch, work 16 sts in original colors; rep from *—112 sts; 28 sts each needle.

RNDS 13–46: Cont in patt from Cable chart, working 2 sts into each ryo for the rest of the pattern—256 sts; 64 sts each needle; piece measures 7½" (19 cm) from CO.

Band

Change to smaller needles and work firmly as foll:

SET-UP RND: Tk1, *[Tp2tog (see Stitch Guide) with B] 2 times, [Tk2tog (see Stitch Guide) with A] 2 times; rep from * to last 7 sts, [Tp2tog with B] 2 times, Tk2tog with A, temporarily sl last st to right needle, remove beg-of-rnd m, return slipped st to left needle, Tk2tog with A (last st tog with Tk1 st after it), replace m—128 sts rem.

NEXT RND: *Tp2 with B, Tk2 with A; rep from *.

Rep the last rnd until band measures 1½" (3.8 cm). Remove the beg-of-rnd m and, with a single yarn of your choice, use Vicki's ribbed method for k2, p2 rib (see page 26) starting with ssk to BO all sts.

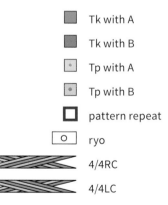

■ Tk with A

■ Tk with B

▫ Tp with A

▫ Tp with B

☐ pattern repeat

⊙ ryo

4/4RC

4/4LC

See Stitch Guide for abbreviations.

Finishing

Weave in loose ends separately and as invisibly as possible (see page 45).

Buttoned HAT & FINGERLESS MITTS

This basic Twigg-stitch hat and matching fingerless mitts are worked flat in rows with three-color stripes. The pieces have buttonholes at each side that are fastened with double buttons (which can be a different style on each side of the fabric), making the entire set completely reversible. For fun, each side features a different stripe pattern. The top of the hat is shaped with decreases that form an interesting star pattern. The thumbs on the mitts are positioned so that there is no "left" or "right" mitt; each can be worn on either hand or with either side facing out.

FINISHED SIZE

Hat: about 19¾" (50 cm) head circumference and 7½" (19 cm) tall, buttoned and unstretched; will stretch to accommodate heads up to 22½" (57 cm).

Mitts: about 7¾ (8½, 9)" (19.5 [21.5, 23] cm) hand circumference, buttoned and unstretched, and 5" (12.5 cm) long. Shown in size 8½" (21.5 cm).

Yarn

Fingering weight (#1 Super Fine).

Shown here: O-Wool Classic 2-Ply (100% certified organic merino; 198 yd [181 m]/50 g): #6403 Haystack (yellow; A), 2 skeins for entire set in any size; #2300 Sky (light blue; B) and #2301 Cornflower (dark blue; C), 1 skein each for entire set in any size.

Note: Each hat requires about 100 yd (91 m) of A and 50 yd (46 m) each of B and C; the mitts shown in the middle size require about 120 yd (110 m) of A and 60 yd (55 m) each of B and C.

Needles

Size U.S. 3 (3.25 mm): straight or circular (cir).

Adjust needle size if necessary to obtain the correct gauge.

Notions

Markers (m), sharp-point tapestry needle; fourteen ½" (1.3 cm) to ⅝" (1.5 cm) buttons (with or without shanks) for hat (seven for each side of the fabric); twenty ½" (1.3 cm) to ⅝" (1.5 cm) buttons (with or without shanks) for mitts (five for each side of the fabric for each mitt).

Gauge

29½ sts and 30½ rows = 4" (10 cm) in Twigg stitch.

Techniques

- ◯ Basic Twigg stitch, page 10.
- ◯ Single-color ribbed-cable cast-on, page 15.
- ◯ Rolled-edge selvedge, page 41.
- ◯ Branched increase, page 39.
- ◯ Vicki's single-color rib bind-off, page 26.

Stitch Guide

Tk: Twigg-knit so that the knit yarn traps the purl yarn.

Tp: Twigg-purl so that the purl yarn traps the knit yarn.

Tk3tog: Twigg-knit 3 sts tog (2 knit stitches plus the purl stitch between them) using the knit yarn.

Tp3tog: Twigg-purl 3 sts tog (2 purl stitches plus the knit stitch between them) using the purl yarn.

ryo: (reverse yarnover) Bring both yarns from back to front over the top of the right needle tip and between the two needles to the back again to create a double-strand loop with a reverse mount. On the following row, work Tk1, Tp1 into the back of the double-strand loop—2 sts made from 2-strand ryo (see page 37).

NOTES

For tidy selvedges, purl the first two stitches of every row and knit the last two stitches of every row as follows: at the beginning of the row, hold the yarns in their knit and purl positions, making sure that they're not crossed over each other, bring both yarns to the front, work a regular purl stitch using the knit color, then work another regular purl stitch with the purl color. Continue in Twigg stitch to the last two stitches, bring both yarns to the back of the work, work a regular knit stitch using the knit color, then work another regular knit stitch using the purl color. ● To change between B and C for the stripe pattern, bring the old yarn up and over the left needle, then hold it at the back of the work, so it lies between the first two stitches. Hold color A and the new yarn ready for the row (without twisting them), purl 1 with A, slip the wrap of the old yarn, purl 1 with the new yarn, then continue in pattern across the row. Doing so will ensure that the "resting" yarn is in position for when it's needed again. ● Work two stitches into the double strand of each ryo by working Tk1 with knit color, then Tp1 with purl color.

Hat

With A, use the single-color ribbed-cable method (see page 15) to CO 148 sts. Join B and C by tying them to the cast-on row a few sts away from the tip of the needle to anchor them (see page 10). Change between B and C as directed every 2 rows as foll:

ROW 1: (knit with A; purl with B) Purl 2 selvedge sts (see Notes), *Tk1, Tp1; rep from * to last 2 sts, knit 2 selvedge sts (see Notes).

ROW 2: (knit with B; purl with A) Purl 2 selvedge sts, *Tk1, Tp1; rep from * to last 2 sts, knit 2 selvedge sts.

ROW 3: (buttonhole row: knit with A; purl with C) Purl 2 selvedge sts, ryo (see Stitch Guide), Tk3tog (see Stitch Guide), Tp1, work as established to last 6 sts, Tk1, Tp3tog (see Stitch Guide), ryo, knit 2 selvedge sts.

ROW 4: (knit with C; purl with A) Purl 2 selvedge sts, work 2 sts in ryo (see Notes), work as established to ryo at other end, work 2 sts in ryo, knit 2 selvedge sts.

ROWS 5 AND 6: Exchange C and B and rep Rows 1 and 2.

ROW 7: (knit with C; purl with A) Purl 2 selvedge sts, work as established to last 2 sts, knit 2 selvedge sts.

ROW 8: (knit with A; purl with C) Purl 2 selvedge sts, work as established to last 2 sts, knit 2 selvedge sts.

Rep Rows 1–8 three more times, then work Rows 1–6 once more—38 rows total; 5 buttonholes completed at each side; piece measures about 5" (12.5 cm) from CO.

> **note:** To adjust the length, work more or fewer repeats of Rows 1–8 before finishing with Rows 1–6; every eight rows added or removed will lengthen or shorten the hat by about 1" (2.5 cm).

Shape Crown

Exchanging colors as before, cont stripe patt and work as foll:

ROW 1: (decrease row: knit with C; purl with A) Purl 2 selvedge sts, place marker (pm), *work 2 sts as established, Tk1, Tp3tog, work 24 sts as established, Tk3tog, Tp1, work 2 sts as established, pm; rep from * 3 more times, knit 2 selvedge sts—132 sts rem: 4 marked sections with 32 sts each and 2 selvedge sts at each side.

Slip markers on foll rows as you come to them.

ROW 2: (knit with A; purl with C) Work even as established, with 2 selvedge sts each side.

ROW 3: (knit with A; purl with B) Work even with 2 selvedge sts each side.

ROW 4: (knit with B; purl with A) Work even with 2 selvedge sts each side.

ROW 5: (decrease and buttonhole row: knit with A; purl with C) Purl 2 selvedge sts, sl m, ryo, Tk3tog, Tp3tog, work 20 sts as established, Tk3tog, Tp1, work 2 sts as established, sl m, *work 2 sts as established, Tk1, Tp3tog, work 20 sts as established, Tk3tog, Tp1, work 2 sts as established, sl m; rep from * once more, work 2 sts as established, Tk1, Tp3tog, work 20 sts as established, Tk3tog, Tp3tog, ryo, sl m, knit 2 selvedge sts—116 sts rem: 4 marked sections with 28 sts each and 2 selvedge sts at each side; 6th buttonhole completed at each side.

ROW 6: (knit with C; purl with A) Purl 2 selvedge sts, work 2 sts in ryo, work as established to ryo at other end, work 2 sts in ryo, knit 2 selvedge sts.

ROW 7: (decrease row: knit with A; purl with B) Purl 2 selvedge sts, sl m, *work 2 sts as established, Tk1, Tp3tog,

work 16 sts as established, Tk3tog, Tp1, work 2 sts as established, sl m; rep from * 3 more times, knit 2 selvedge sts—100 sts rem: 4 marked sections with 24 sts each and 2 selvedge sts at each side.

ROW 8: (knit with B; purl with A) Work even with 2 selvedge sts each side.

ROW 9: (decrease row: knit with C; purl with A) Purl 2 selvedge sts, sl m, *work 2 sts as established, Tk1, Tp3tog, work 12 sts as established, Tk3tog, Tp1, work 2 sts as established, sl m; rep from * 3 more times, knit 2 selvedge sts—84 sts rem: 4 marked sections with 20 sts each and 2 selvedge sts at each side.

ROW 10: (knit with A; purl with C) Work even with 2 selvedge sts each side.

ROW 11: (decrease row: knit with A; purl with B) Purl 2 selvedge sts, sl m, *work 2 sts as established, Tk1, Tp3tog, work 8 sts as established, Tk3tog, Tp1, work 2 sts as established, sl m; rep from * 3 more times, knit 2 selvedge sts—68 sts rem: 4 marked sections with 16 sts each and 2 selvedge sts at each side.

ROW 12: (knit with B; purl with A) Work even with 2 selvedge sts each side.

ROW 13: (decrease and buttonhole row: knit with A; purl with C) Purl 2 selvedge sts, sl m, ryo, Tk3tog, Tp3tog, work 4 sts as established, Tk3tog, Tp1, work 2 sts as established, sl m, *work 2 sts as established, Tk1,

Tp3tog, work 4 sts as established, Tk3tog, Tp1, work 2 sts as established, sl m; rep from * once more, work 2 sts as established, Tk1, Tp3tog, work 4 sts as established, Tk3tog, Tp3tog, ryo, sl m, knit 2 selvedge sts—52 sts rem: 4 marked sections with 12 sts each and 2 selvedge sts at each side; 7th buttonhole completed at each side.

ROW 14: (knit with C; purl with A) Work even with 2 selvedge sts each side.

ROW 15: (decrease row: knit with A; purl with B) Purl 2 selvedge sts, sl m, *work 2 sts as established, Tk1, Tp3tog, Tk3tog, Tp1, work 2 sts as established, sl m; rep from * 3 more times, knit 2 selvedge sts—36 sts rem: 4 marked sections with 8 sts each and 2 selvedge sts at each side.

ROW 16: (knit with B; purl with A) Work even with 2 selvedge sts each side.

ROW 17: (knit with C; purl with A) Work even with 2 selvedge sts each side.

ROW 18: (knit with A; purl with C) Work even with 2 selvedge sts each side—piece measures about 7½" (19 cm) from CO.

Cut yarns, leaving 8" (20.5 cm) tails. Thread C on a tapestry needle and draw through the C sts; thread A on a tapestry needle and draw through the A sts. Remove the needles, pull each yarn tight, and secure the ends.

Finishing

Weave in loose ends separately and as invisibly as possible (see page 45).

Buttons

Sew or tie the buttons together in pairs, back-to-back; this allows you to button the hat with either side as the "public" side. If the buttons have no shanks, sew or tie them loosely to leave up to ½" (1.3 cm) slack between the buttons in each pair. You may find it helpful to apply a dab of glue to secure the thread or yarn used to attach the buttons. Overlap the buttonhole edge with the desired side facing out and button the hat closed through both layers as shown.

Mitts

With A, use the single-color ribbed-cable method (see page 15) to CO 56 (60, 64) sts. Join B and C by tying them to the cast-on row a few sts away from the tip of the needle to anchor them (see page 10). Change between B and C as directed every 2 rows.

ROW 1: (knit with A; purl with B) Purl 2 selvedge sts (see Notes), *Tk1, Tp1; rep from * to last 2 sts, knit 2 selvedge sts (see Notes).

ROW 2: (knit with B; purl with A) Purl 2 selvedge sts, *Tk1, Tp1; rep from * to last 2 sts, knit 2 selvedge sts.

ROW 3: (buttonhole row: knit with A; purl with C) Purl 2 selvedge sts, ryo (see Stitch Guide), Tk3tog (see Stitch Guide), Tp1, work as established to last 6 sts, Tk1, Tp3tog (see Stitch Guide), ryo, knit 2 selvedge sts.

ROW 4: (knit with C; purl with A) Purl 2 selvedge sts, work 2 sts in ryo (see Notes), work as established to ryo at the other end, work 2 sts in ryo, knit 2 selvedge sts.

ROWS 5 AND 6: Exchange C and B and rep Rows 1 and 2—piece measures about ¾" (2 cm) from CO.

Shape Thumb Gusset

ROW 7: (increase row: knit with C; purl with A) Purl 2 selvedge sts, work 24 (26, 28) sts as established, place marker (pm), use the branched method (see page 39) to [increase the next 2-st rib to 4 sts] 2 times, pm, work 24 (26, 28) sts as established, knit 2 selvedge sts—4 sts inc'd; 8 gusset sts between m.

Slip markers (sl m) on the foll rows as you come to them.

ROW 8: (knit with A; purl with C) Work as established, working new sts in patt.

ROW 9: (knit with A; purl with B) Work as established.

ROW 10: (knit with B; purl with A) Work as established.

ROW 11: (increase and buttonhole row: knit with A; purl with C) Purl 2 selvedge sts, ryo, Tk3tog, Tp1, work as established to first gusset m, sl m, work branched inc in next 2-st rib, work 4 sts as established, work branched inc in next 2-st rib, sl m, work as established to last 6 sts, Tk1, Tp3tog, ryo, knit 2 selvedge sts—4 sts inc'd; 12 gusset sts between m.

ROW 12: (knit with C; purl with A) Purl 2 selvedge sts, work 2 sts in ryo, work as established to ryo at the other end, work 2 sts in ryo, knit 2 selvedge sts.

ROW 13: (knit with A; purl with B) Work as established.

ROW 14: (knit with B; purl with A) Work as established.

ROW 15: (increase row: knit with C; purl with A) Purl 2 selvedge sts, work as established to first gusset m, sl m, work branched inc in next 2-st rib, work 8 sts as established, work branched inc in next 2-st rib, sl m, work as established to last 2 sts, knit 2 selvedge sts—4 sts inc'd; 16 gusset sts between m.

ROW 16: (knit with A; purl with C) Work as established.

ROW 17: (knit with A; purl with B) Work as established.

ROW 18: (knit with B; purl with A) Work as established.

ROW 19: (increase and buttonhole row; knit with A; purl with C) Purl 2 selvedge sts, ryo, Tk3tog, Tp1, work as established to first gusset m, sl m, work branched inc in next 2-st rib, work 12 sts as established, work branched inc in next 2-st rib, sl m, work as established to last 6 sts, Tk1, Tp3tog, ryo, knit 2 selvedge sts—4 sts inc'd; 20 gusset sts between m.

ROW 20: (knit with C; purl with A) Purl 2 selvedge sts, work 2 sts in ryo, work as established to ryo at the other end, work 2 sts in ryo, knit 2 selvedge sts.

ROW 21: (knit with A; purl with B) Work as established.

ROW 22: (knit with B; purl with A) Work as established.

ROW 23: (increase row: knit with C; purl with A) Purl 2 selvedge sts, work as established to first gusset m, sl m, work branched inc in next 2-st rib, work 16 sts as established, work branched inc in next 2-st rib, sl m, work as established to last 2 sts, knit 2 selvedge sts—4 sts inc'd; 24 gusset sts between m.

ROW 24: (knit with A; purl with C) Work as established.

ROW 25: (knit with A; purl with B) Work as established.

ROW 26: (knit with B; purl with A) Work as established.

ROW 27: (increase and buttonhole row: knit with A; purl with C) Purl 2 selvedge sts, ryo, Tk3tog, Tp1, work as established to first gusset m, sl m, work branched inc in next 2-st rib, work 20 sts as established, work branched inc in next 2-st rib, sl m, work as established to last 6 sts, Tk1, Tp3tog, ryo, knit 2 selvedge sts—80 (84, 88) sts total; 28 gusset sts between m.

ROW 28: (knit with C; purl with A) Purl 2 selvedge sts, work 2 sts in ryo, work as established to ryo at other end, work 2 sts in ryo, knit 2 selvedge sts—piece measures about 3¾" (9.5 cm) from CO.

Top of Thumb

ROW 29: (knit with A; purl with B) Purl 2 selvedge sts, then slipping the first gusset m, work 50 (52, 54) sts as established to 2 sts before second gusset m. Using e-wrap loops, make 1 st with A, then 1 st with B. Turn work so other side is facing, work the new sts as knit with B, purl with A, then work 24 thumb sts as established, ending 2 sts before m. Using e-wrap loops, make 1 st with B then 1 st with A. Turn work and, using A only, work [k1, p1] 14 times across the 28 thumb gusset sts. Turn work and use Vicki's single-color rib method (see page 26) beginning with ssk and ending with p3tog to BO 28 gusset sts. Cut both yarns, leaving 6" (15 cm) tails. Turn work to continue, then make a slipknot with both yarns to anchor them and place the slipknot on the right needle. Cont across Row 29 in established patt (removing rem m when you come to it), work as established to last 2 sts, knit 2 selvedge sts—56 (60, 64) sts rem, arranged in 2 sets of 28 (30, 32) sts on each side of thumb.

ROW 30: (knit with B; purl with A) Purl 2 selvedge sts, work 26 (28, 30) sts to thumb opening, drop the slipknot. Pick up 2 sts from the base of the extra sts on the thumb by picking up 1 st knitwise with B, and 1 st purlwise with A. Hold the 2 groups of sts side by side and pick up 2 more sts in the same way from the extra sts on the other side of the thumb, work 26 (28, 30) sts as established, knit 2 selvedge sts—60 (64, 68) sts total.

Top of Hand

ROW 31: (knit with C; purl with A) Work as established.

ROW 32: (knit with A; purl with C) Work as established.

ROW 33: (knit with A; purl with B) Work as established.

ROW 34: (knit with B; purl with A) Work as established.

ROW 35: (buttonhole row: knit with A; purl with C) Purl 2 selvedge sts, ryo, Tk3tog, Tp1, work as established to last 6 sts, Tk1, Tp3tog, ryo, knit 2 selvedge sts—5 buttonholes completed at each side.

ROW 36: (knit with C; purl with A) Work as established.

ROW 37: (knit with A; purl with B) Work as established.

ROW 38: (knit with B; purl with A) Work as established— piece measures about 5" (12.5 cm) from CO.

With A only, purl 2 selvedge sts, work in k1, p1 rib to last 2 sts, knit 2 selvedge sts. Use Vicki's single-color rib method beginning with ssk to BO all sts.

Finishing

Use the ends at the top of the thumb to join the two sides of the thumb together and close any gaps.

Weave in loose ends separately and as invisibly as possible (see page 45).

Buttons

Join buttons together in pairs as for hat. Button each mitt closed through both layers as for hat.

Fan SHAWL

Rows of Twigg stitch fans are stacked one on top of another in nine tiers for this wide, shallow geometric shawl. The first tier begins with a twined-cable cast-on, then three fans are worked in basic Twigg stitch. Each successive tier contains one additional fan, and the fans gradually increase in size to create a gently curved shape. A two-color stretchy chain bind-off ensures that the outer edge remains loose and flexible. Although this shawl appears complicated, each fan follows a simple, basic plan that's easy to memorize.

FINISHED SIZE

About 60" (152.5 cm) measured along outer curve at lower edge (see Notes) and 10½" (26.5 cm) high in center.

Yarn

Fingering weight (#1 Super Fine).

Shown here: Manos del Uruguay Fino (70% extrafine merino, 30% silk; 490 yd [450 m]/100 g): #404 Watered Silk (light; A) and #405 Peacock Plume (dark; B), 1 skein each.

Note: One shawl requires about 300 yd [274 m] of each color.

Needles

Size U.S. 3 (3.25 mm).

Adjust needle size if necessary to obtain the correct gauge.

Notions

Stitch markers (m); sharp-point tapestry needle.

Gauge

Tier 1 smallest fans (18 sts wide and 7 rows high) measure about 1¾" (4.5 cm) wide and 1¼" (3.2 cm) tall.

Tier 9 largest fans (50 sts wide and 23 rows high) measure about 5¼" (13.5 cm) wide and 3" (7.5 cm) tall.

Techniques

NOTES

The finished measurements include all the stitches—the fans themselves as well as the selvedge stitches at each side and the stitches between the fan motifs. ● The two colors exchange positions on alternate tiers, so the Stitch Guide fan instructions simply refer to the knit and purl yarns. The directions for each tier specify how to use the colors for that entire tier. ● The shawl begins with three fans in the first tier and adds one more fan in each successive tier to end with eleven fans in the ninth tier. The diagram on page 84 shows only Tiers 1–4. ● The fans gradually increase in size so that the fans of each tier are four stitches wider (at their widest point) and two rows taller than the fans of the previous tier. ● Two stitches are worked between each pair of fans and between the end fans and the selvedges, which will become the foundation stitches for the fans of the following tier. ● For tidy selvedges at each end of each tier, purl the first two edge stitches and knit the last two edge stitches as follows: for the two edge stitches at the beginning of the row, make sure that the yarns are not crossed over each other, bring both yarns to the front, work a regular purl stitch using the knit color, then work another regular purl stitch with the purl color. For the two edge stitches at the end of a tier, bring both yarns to the back of the work, work a regular knit stitch using the knit color, then work another regular knit stitch using the purl color. ● Work [Tk1 with knit color, Tp1 with purl color] into the double strand of each ryo, unless otherwise specified. ● The decreases on the charts join each fan to the surrounding live stitches as it is worked. The first fan on each tier uses only the gold-outlined decreases at the left-hand side of the charts to join at the end of odd-numbered rows. The middle fans use the red- and gold-outlined decreases on both sides of the charts. The last fan uses only the red-outlined decreases at the right-hand side of the charts to join at the beginning of odd-numbered rows. ● You can continue to add more tiers as desired for a larger shawl; keep in mind that doing so will require more yarn.

Stitch Guide

Tk: Twigg-knit so that the knit yarn traps the purl yarn.

Tp: Twigg-purl so that the purl yarn traps the knit yarn.

Tk3tog: Twigg-knit 3 stitches together (2 knit stitches plus the purl stitch between them) using the knit yarn.

Tp3tog: Twigg-purl 3 stitches together (2 purl stitches plus the knit stitch between them) using the purl yarn.

slip 2: Sl 1 st with both yarns in back, then sl 1 st with both yarns in front.

ryo: (reverse yarnover) Bring both yarns from back to front over the top of the right needle tip and between the two needles to the back again to create a double-strand loop with a reverse mount. On the following row, work Tk1, Tp1 into the back of the double-strand loop—2 sts made from 2-strand ryo (see page 37).

FIRST FAN OF EACH TIER

See tier directions for knit and purl color assignments.

Row 1: Purl 2 selvedge sts (see Notes), work Row 1 of chart by working double-rib branched inc (see page 39) in next 2 sts to inc them to 6 sts, turn work.

Row 2: Work Row 2 of chart to last 2 sts, knit 2 selvedge sts.

Row 3: Purl 2 selvedge sts, work Row 3 to last chart st, work gold-outlined Tp3tog as shown (last fan st tog with next 2 sts after it; see Stitch Guide), turn work.

Row 4: Work Row 4 of chart to last 2 sts, knit 2 selvedge sts.

Rows 5 to end: Cont in chart patt, working 2 selvedge sts as established and working dec joins at end of odd-numbered rows, and ending with the row number given for your tier.

MIDDLE FAN(S) OF EACH TIER

See tier directions for knit and purl color assignments.

Work set-up sts as directed.

Row 1: Work Row 1 of chart by working double branched-rib inc in next 2 sts to inc them to 6 sts as shown on chart, turn work.

Row 2: Work Row 2 of chart, slip 2 (see Stitch Guide), turn work.

Row 3: Work Row 3 of chart, working red-outlined Tk3tog as shown (2 sl sts tog with 1 fan st after them; see Stitch Guide), work to last chart st, work gold-outlined Tp3tog as shown (last fan st tog with next 2 sts), turn work.

Row 4: Work Row 4 of chart, slip 2, turn work.

Rows 5 to end: Cont in chart patt, working dec joins at both ends of odd-numbered rows and 2 slipped sts at end of even-numbered rows, ending with the row number given for your tier.

LAST FAN OF EACH TIER

See tier directions for knit and purl color assignments.

Work set-up sts as directed.

Row 1: Work Row 1 of chart by working double branched-rib inc in next 2 sts to inc them to 6 sts as shown on chart, knit 2 selvedge sts.

Row 2: Purl 2 selvedge sts, work Row 2 of chart, slip 2, turn work.

Row 3: Work red-outlined Tk3tog as shown (2 sl sts tog with 1 fan st after them), work to end of chart, knit 2 selvedge sts.

Row 4: Purl 2 selvedge sts, work Row 4 of chart, slip 2, turn work.

Row 5 to end: Cont in chart patt, working dec joins at beg of odd-numbered rows, 2 slipped sts at end of even-numbered rows, and 2 selvedge sts as established, ending with the row number given for your tier.

Shawl

Use the twined-cable method (see page 18) to CO 12 sts, pm, CO 16 sts, pm, CO 10 sts—38 sts total.

Tier 1 (A side facing)

Knit with A and purl with B on odd-numbered rows; knit with B and purl with A on even-numbered rows. This tier contains three fans (one first, one middle, and one last) worked in pattern from the Odd Tiers Fan chart.

FIRST FAN

For this fan, work the red-outlined sts as Tk1 with A and work the gold-outlined sts as Tp3tog with B to join 1 fan st to the next 2 sts after it. Work short-rows over the first 10-st group (the last sts CO) according to the First Fan instructions (see Stitch Guide) until Row 6 of chart has been completed.

ROW 7: Purl 2 selvedge sts, work lifted inc (see page 38) to inc 2 sts from strands between the needles, work to last chart st, Tp3tog (last fan st tog with next 2 sts), re-move m, do not turn work—22 worked sts on right needle: 2 selvedge sts, 2 inc'd foundation sts for next tier, 18 fan sts; 28 unworked sts rem on left needle.

MIDDLE FAN

For this fan, work the red-outlined sts as Tk3tog with A to join 1 fan st to 2 slipped sts and work the gold-outlined sts as Tp3tog with B to join 1 fan st to the next 2 sts after it.

SET-UP: With A side still facing, [Tk1, Tp1] 4 times to center of 16 marked sts, do not turn work.

Work short-rows according to the Middle Fan instructions (see Stitch Guide) until Row 6 of chart has been completed.

ROW 7: Tk3tog (2 sl sts tog with 1 fan st after them), work to last chart st, Tp3tog (last fan st tog with next 2 sts), remove m, do not turn work—42 worked sts on right needle: 2 selvedge sts, [2 foundation sts, 18 fan sts] 2 times; 12 unworked sts rem on left needle.

LAST FAN

For this fan, work the red-outlined sts as Tk3tog with A to join 1 fan st to 2 slipped sts and work the gold-outlined sts as Tp1 with B.

SET-UP: With A side still facing, [Tk1, Tp1] 4 times to last 4 sts, do not turn work.

Dropping CO slipknot from needle as you come to it, work short-rows over rem group of sts according to the Last Fan instructions (see Stitch Guide) until Row 6 of chart has been completed.

ROW 7: Tk3tog (2 sl sts tog with 1 fan st after them), work to end of chart, work lifted inc, knit 2 selvedge sts—66 sts total: read from right to left with light side facing, 2 selvedge sts, [2 foundation sts, 18 fan sts] 3 times, 2 foundation sts, 2 selvedge sts.

Tier 2 (B side facing)

Knit with B and purl with A on odd-numbered rows; knit with A and purl with B on even-numbered rows. This tier contains four fans (one first, two middle, and one last) worked in pattern from the Even Tiers Fan chart.

Turn work so B (dark) side is facing.

☐	Tk with A on odd rows; Tp with A on even rows
▨	Tk with B on odd rows; Tp with B on even rows
·	Tp with A on odd rows; Tk with A on even rows
·	Tp with B on odd rows; Tk with B on even rows
⤬	Tk3tog with A for middle and last fans; Tk with A for first fan
⤬	Tk3tog with B for middle and last fans; Tk with B for first fan
⤬	Tp3tog with A for first and middle fans; Tp with A for last fan
⤬	Tp3tog with B for first and middle fans; Tp with B for last fan
☐ ■	outlined sts worked differently in first, middle, and last fans (see instructions)
o	ryo
⟆	double branched rib inc (6 sts made from 2 sts)

See Stitch Guide for abbreviations.

ODD TIERS FAN

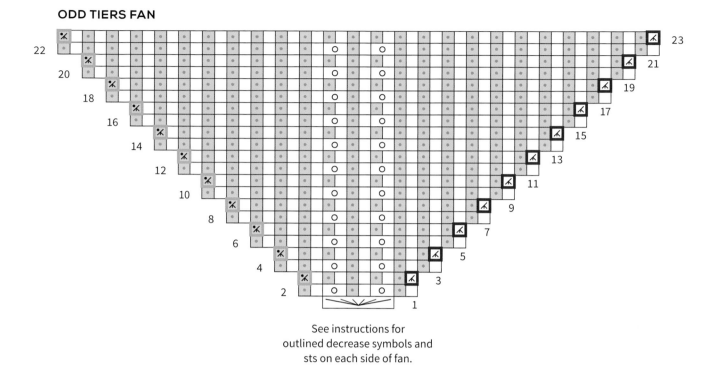

See instructions for
outlined decrease symbols and
sts on each side of fan.

EVEN TIERS FAN

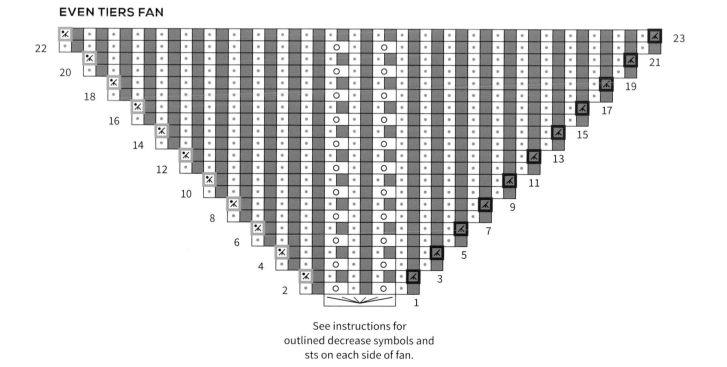

See instructions for
outlined decrease symbols and
sts on each side of fan.

FIRST FAN

For this fan, work the red-outlined sts as Tk1 with B and work the gold-outlined sts as Tp3tog with A to join 1 fan st to the next 2 sts after it. Work short-rows according to First Fan instructions until Row 8 of chart has been completed.

ROW 9: Purl 2 selvedge sts, work lifted inc, work to last chart st, Tp3tog (last fan st tog with next 2 sts), do not turn work—26 worked sts on right needle: 2 selvedge sts, 2 inc'd foundation sts for next tier, 22 fan sts; 54 unworked sts rem on left needle.

MIDDLE FANS (MAKE 2)

For these fans, work the red-outlined sts as Tk3tog with B to join 1 fan st to 2 slipped sts and work the gold-outlined sts as Tp3tog with A to join 1 fan st to the next 2 sts after it.

SET-UP: With B side still facing, [Tk1, Tp1] 5 times, do not turn work.

Work short-rows according to Middle Fan instructions until Row 8 of chart has been completed.

ROW 9: Tk3tog (2 sl sts tog with 1 fan st after them), work to last chart st, Tp3tog (last fan st tog with next 2 sts), do not turn work—50 worked sts on right needle: 2 selvedge sts, [2 foundation sts, 22 fan sts] 2 times; 34 unworked sts rem on left needle.

For the second middle fan, work set-up row again, then work Rows 1–9 once more—74 worked sts on right needle: 2 selvedge sts, [2 foundation sts, 22 fan sts] 3 times; 14 unworked sts rem on left needle.

LAST FAN

For this fan, work the red-outlined sts as Tk3tog with B to join 1 fan st to 2 slipped sts and work the gold-outlined sts as Tp1 with A.

SET-UP: With B side still facing, [Tk1, Tp1] 5 times to last 4 sts, do not turn work.

Work short-rows according to the Last Fan instructions until Row 8 of chart has been completed.

ROW 9: Tk3tog (2 sl sts tog with 1 fan st after them), work to end of chart, work lifted inc, knit 2 selvedge sts—102

FAN SHAWL DIAGRAM

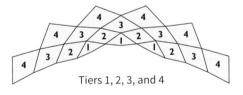

Tiers 1, 2, 3, and 4

sts total: read from right to left with dark side facing 2 selvedge sts, [2 foundation sts, 22 fan sts] 4 times, 2 foundation sts, 2 selvedge sts.

Tier 3 (A side facing)

Knit with A and purl with B on odd-numbered rows; knit with B and purl with A on even-numbered rows. This tier contains five fans (one first, three middle, and one last) worked in pattern from the Odd Tiers Fan chart.

Turn work so A (light) side is facing.

FIRST FAN

Work short-rows according to First Fan instructions until Row 10 of chart has been completed.

ROW 11: Purl 2 selvedge sts, work lifted inc, work to last chart st, Tp3tog (last fan st tog with next 2 sts), do not turn work—30 worked sts on right needle: 2 selvedge sts, 2 inc'd foundation sts for next tier, 26 fan sts; 88 unworked sts rem on left needle.

MIDDLE FANS (MAKE 3)

SET-UP: With light side still facing, [Tk1, Tp1] 6 times, do not turn work.

Work short-rows according to Middle Fan instructions until Row 10 of chart has been completed.

ROW 11: Tk3tog (2 sl sts tog with 1 fan st after them), work to last chart st, Tp3tog (last fan st tog with next 2 sts), do not turn work—58 worked sts on right needle; 64 unworked sts rem on left needle.

For the next two middle fans, *work set-up row, then work Rows 1–11; rep from * once more.

After the second middle fan, there will be 86 worked sts on right needle; 40 unworked sts on left needle.

After the third middle fan, there will be 114 worked sts on right needle; 16 unworked sts on left needle.

LAST FAN

SET-UP: With A side still facing, [Tk1, Tp1] 6 times to last 4 sts, do not turn work.

Work short-rows according to Last Fan instructions until Row 10 of chart has been completed.

ROW 11: Tk3tog (2 sl sts tog with 1 fan st after them), work to end of chart, work lifted inc, knit 2 selvedge sts—146 sts total: read from right to left with light side facing, 2 selvedge sts, [2 foundation sts, 26 fan sts] 5 times, 2 foundation sts, 2 selvedge sts.

Tier 4 (B side facing)

Knit with B and purl with A on odd-numbered rows; knit with A and purl with B on even-numbered rows. This tier contains six fans (one first, four middle, and one last) worked in pattern from the Even Tiers Fan chart.

Turn work so B (dark) side is facing.

FIRST FAN

Work short-rows according to First Fan instructions until Row 12 of chart has been completed.

ROW 13: Purl 2 selvedge sts, work lifted inc, work to last chart st, Tp3tog (last fan st tog with next 2 sts), do not turn work—34 worked sts on right needle; 130 unworked sts rem on left needle.

MIDDLE FANS (MAKE 4)

SET-UP: With B side still facing, [Tk1, Tp1] 7 times, do not turn work.

Work short-rows according to Middle Fan instructions until Row 12 of chart has been completed.

ROW 13: Tk3tog (2 sl sts tog with 1 fan st after them), work to last chart st, Tp3tog (last fan st tog with next 2 sts), do not turn work—66 worked sts on right needle; 102 unworked sts rem on left needle.

For the next three middle fans, *work set-up row, then work Rows 1–13; rep from * 2 more times.

After the second middle fan, there will be 98 worked sts on right needle; 74 unworked sts on left needle.

After the third middle fan, there will be 130 worked sts on right needle; 46 unworked sts on left needle.

After the fourth middle fan, there will be 162 worked sts on right needle; 18 unworked sts on left needle.

LAST FAN

SET-UP: With B side still facing, [Tk1, Tp1] 7 times to last 4 sts, do not turn work.

Work short-rows according to Last Fan instructions until Row 12 of chart has been completed.

ROW 13: Tk3tog (2 sl sts tog with 1 fan st after them), work to end of chart, work lifted inc, knit 2 selvedge sts—198 sts total: read from right to left with dark side facing, 2 selvedge sts, [2 foundation sts, 30 fan sts] 6 times, 2 foundation sts, 2 selvedge sts.

Tier 5 (A side facing)

Knit with A and purl with B on odd-numbered rows; knit with B and purl with A on even-numbered rows. This tier contains seven fans (one first, five middle, and one last) worked in pattern from the Odd Tiers Fan chart.

Turn work so A (light) side is facing.

FIRST FAN

Work short-rows according to First Fan instructions until Row 14 of chart has been completed.

ROW 15: Purl 2 selvedge sts, work lifted inc, work to last chart st, Tp3tog (last fan st tog with next 2 sts), do not turn work—38 worked sts on right needle; 180 unworked sts rem on left needle.

MIDDLE FANS (MAKE 5)

SET-UP: With A side still facing, work [Tk1, Tp1] 8 times, do not turn work.

Work short-rows according to Middle Fan instructions until Row 14 of chart has been completed.

ROW 15: Tk3tog (2 sl sts tog with 1 fan st after them), work to last chart st, Tp3tog (last fan st tog with next 2 sts), do not turn work—74 worked sts on right needle; 148 unworked sts rem on left needle.

For the next four middle fans, *work set-up row, then work Rows 1–15; rep from * 3 more times.

After the second middle fan, there will be 110 worked sts on right needle; 116 unworked sts on left needle.

After the third middle fan, there will be 146 worked sts on right needle; 84 unworked sts on left needle.

After the fourth middle fan, there will be 182 worked sts on right needle; 52 unworked sts on left needle.

After the fifth middle fan, there will be 218 worked sts on right needle; 20 unworked sts on left needle.

LAST FAN

SET-UP: With A side still facing, [Tk1, Tp1] 8 times to last 4 sts, do not turn work.

Work short-rows according to Last Fan instructions until Row 14 of chart has been completed.

ROW 15: Tk3tog (2 sl sts tog with 1 fan st after them), work to end of chart, work lifted inc, knit 2 selvedge sts—258 sts total: read from right to left with light side facing 2 selvedge sts, [2 foundation sts, 34 fan sts] 7 times, 2 foundation sts, 2 selvedge sts.

Tier 6 (B side facing)

Knit with B and purl with A on odd-numbered rows; knit with A and purl with B on even-numbered rows. This tier contains eight fans (one first, six middle, and one last) worked in pattern from the Even Tiers Fan chart.

Turn work so B (dark) side is facing.

FIRST FAN

Work short-rows according to First Fan instructions until Row 16 of chart has been completed.

ROW 17: Purl 2 selvedge sts, work lifted inc, work to last chart st, Tp3tog (last fan st tog with next 2 sts), do not turn work—42 worked sts on right needle; 238 unworked sts rem on left needle.

MIDDLE FANS (MAKE 6)

SET-UP: With B side still facing, [Tk1, Tp1] 9 times, do not turn work.

Work short-rows according to Middle Fan instructions until Row 16 of chart has been completed.

ROW 17: Tk3tog (2 sl sts tog with 1 fan st after them), work to last chart st, Tp3tog (last fan st tog with next 2 sts), do not turn work—82 worked sts on right needle; 202 unworked sts rem on left needle.

For the next five middle fans, *work set-up row, then work Rows 1–17; rep from * 4 more times.

After the second middle fan, there will be 122 worked sts on right needle; 166 unworked sts on left needle.

After the third middle fan, there will be 162 worked sts on right needle; 130 unworked sts on left needle.

After the fourth middle fan, there will be 202 worked sts on right needle; 94 unworked sts on left needle.

After the fifth middle fan, there will be 242 worked sts on right needle; 58 unworked sts on left needle.

After the sixth middle fan, there will be 282 worked sts on right needle; 22 unworked sts on left needle.

LAST FAN

SET-UP: With B side still facing, [Tk1, Tp1] 9 times to last 4 sts, do not turn work.

Work short-rows according to Last Fan instructions until Row 16 of chart has been completed.

ROW 17: Tk3tog (2 sl sts tog with 1 fan st after them), work to end of chart, work lifted inc, knit 2 selvedge sts—326 sts total: read from right to left with dark side facing, 2 selvedge sts, [2 foundation sts, 38 fan sts] 8 times, 2 foundation sts, 2 selvedge sts.

Tier 7 (A side facing)

Knit with A and purl with B on odd-numbered rows; knit with B and purl with A on even-numbered rows. This tier contains nine fans (one first, seven middle, and one last) worked in pattern from the Odd Tiers Fan chart.

Turn work so A (light) side is facing.

FIRST FAN

Work short-rows according to First Fan instructions until Row 18 of chart has been completed.

ROW 19: Purl 2 selvedge sts, work lifted inc, work to last chart st, Tp3tog (last fan st tog with next 2 sts), do not turn work—46 worked sts on right needle; 304 unworked sts rem on left needle.

MIDDLE FANS (MAKE 7)

SET-UP: With A side still facing, [Tk1, Tp1] 10 times, do not turn work.

Work short-rows according to Middle Fan instructions until Row 18 of chart has been completed.

ROW 19: Tk3tog (2 sl sts tog with 1 fan st after them), work to last chart st, Tp3tog (last fan st tog with next 2 sts), do not turn work—90 worked sts on right needle; 264 unworked sts rem on left needle.

For the next six middle fans, *work set-up row, then work Rows 1–19; rep from * 5 more times.

After the second middle fan, there will be 134 worked sts on right needle; 224 unworked sts on left needle.

After the third middle fan, there will be 178 worked sts on right needle; 184 unworked sts on left needle.

After the fourth middle fan, there will be 222 worked sts on right needle; 144 unworked sts on left needle.

After the fifth middle fan, there will be 266 worked sts on right needle; 104 unworked sts on left needle.

After the sixth middle fan, there will be 310 worked sts on right needle; 64 unworked sts on left needle.

After the seventh middle fan, there will be 354 worked sts on right needle; 24 unworked sts on left needle.

LAST FAN

SET-UP: With light side still facing, [Tk1, Tp1] 10 times to last 4 sts, do not turn work.

Work short-rows according to Last Fan instructions until Row 18 of chart has been completed.

ROW 19: Tk3tog (2 sl sts tog with 1 fan st after them), work to end of chart, work lifted inc, knit 2 selvedge sts—402 sts total: read from right to left with light side facing, 2 selvedge sts, [2 foundation sts, 42 fan sts] 9 times, 2 foundation sts, 2 selvedge sts.

Tier 8 (B side facing)

Knit with B and purl with A on odd-numbered rows; knit with A and purl with B on even-numbered rows. This tier contains ten fans (one first, eight middle, and one last) worked in pattern from the Even Tiers Fan chart.

Turn work so B (dark) side is facing.

FIRST FAN

Work short-rows according to First Fan instructions until Row 20 of chart has been completed.

ROW 21: Purl 2 selvedge sts, work lifted inc, work to last chart st, Tp3tog (last fan st tog with next 2 sts), do not turn work—50 worked sts on right needle; 378 unworked sts rem on left needle.

MIDDLE FANS (MAKE 8)

SET-UP: With B side still facing, [Tk1, Tp1] 11 times, do not turn work.

Work short-rows according to Middle Fan instructions until Row 20 of chart has been completed.

ROW 21: Tk3tog (2 sl sts tog with 1 fan st after them), work to last chart st, Tp3tog (last fan st tog with next 2 sts), do not turn work—98 worked sts on right needle; 334 unworked sts rem on left needle.

For the next seven middle fans, *work set-up row, then work Rows 1–21; rep from * 6 more times.

After the second middle fan, there will be 146 worked sts on right needle; 290 unworked sts on left needle.

After the third middle fan, there will be 194 worked sts on right needle; 246 unworked sts on left needle.

After the fourth middle fan, there will be 242 worked sts on right needle; 202 unworked sts on left needle.

After the fifth middle fan, there will be 290 worked sts on right needle; 158 unworked sts on left needle.

After the sixth middle fan, there will be 338 worked sts on right needle; 114 unworked sts on left needle.

After the seventh middle fan, there will be 386 worked sts on right needle; 70 unworked sts on left needle.

After the eighth middle fan, there will be 434 worked sts on right needle; 26 unworked sts on left needle.

LAST FAN

SET-UP: With B side still facing, [Tk1, Tp1] 11 times to last 4 sts, do not turn work.

Work short-rows according to Last Fan instructions until Row 20 of chart has been completed.

ROW 21: Tk3tog (2 sl sts tog with 1 fan st after them), work to end of chart, work lifted inc, knit 2 selvedge sts—486 sts total: 2 selvedge sts, [2 foundation sts, 46 fan sts] 10 times, 2 foundation sts, 2 selvedge sts.

Tier 9 (A side facing)

Knit with A and purl with B on odd-numbered rows; knit with B and purl with A on even-numbered rows. This tier contains eleven fans (one first, nine middle, and one last)

worked in pattern from the Odd Tiers Fan chart, except for Rows 17 and 21, which are worked with the colors reversed for accent stripes. The first and last fans of this tier do not have lifted increases inside the selvedge sts in Row 23.

Turn work so A (light) side is facing.

FIRST FAN

ROWS 1–16: Work short-rows according to First Fan instructions until Row 16 of chart has been completed.

ROW 17: Switch colors (knit with B, purl with A) and work in established patt.

ROWS 18–20: Change back to original colors and work 3 rows in patt.

ROW 21: Switch colors (knit with B, purl with A) and work in established patt.

ROW 22: Change back to original colors and work 1 row in patt.

ROW 23: Work 2 purl selvedge sts, work to last chart st, Tp3tog (last fan st tog with next 2 sts), do not turn work—52 worked sts on right needle; 460 unworked sts rem on left needle.

MIDDLE FANS (MAKE 9)

SET-UP: With A side still facing, [Tk1, Tp1] 12 times, do not turn work.

ROWS 1–16: Work short-rows according to Middle Fan instructions until Row 16 of chart has been completed.

ROW 17: Switch colors (knit with B, purl with A) and work in established patt.

ROWS 18–20: Change back to original colors and work 3 rows in patt.

ROW 21: Switch colors (knit with B, purl with A) and work in established patt.

ROW 22: Change back to original colors and work 1 row in patt.

ROW 23: Tk3tog (2 sl sts tog with 1 fan st after them), work to last chart st, Tp3tog (last fan st tog with next 2 sts), do not turn work—104 worked sts on right needle; 412 unworked sts rem on left needle.

For the next eight middle fans, *work set-up row, then work Rows 1–23; rep from * 7 more times.

After the second middle fan, there will be 156 worked sts on right needle; 364 unworked sts on left needle.

After the third middle fan, there will be 208 worked sts on right needle; 316 unworked sts on left needle.

After the fourth middle fan, there will be 260 worked sts on right needle; 268 unworked sts on left needle.

After the fifth middle fan, there will be 312 worked sts on right needle; 220 unworked sts on left needle.

After the sixth middle fan, there will be 364 worked sts on right needle; 172 unworked sts on left needle.

After the seventh middle fan, there will be 416 worked sts on right needle; 124 unworked sts on left needle.

After the eighth middle fan, there will be 468 worked sts on right needle; 76 unworked sts on left needle.

After the ninth middle fan, there will be 520 worked sts on right needle; 28 unworked sts on left needle.

LAST FAN

SET-UP: With odd-numbered side still facing, [Tk1, Tp1] 12 times to last 4 sts, do not turn work.

ROWS 1–16: Work short-rows according to Last Fan instructions until Row 16 of chart has been completed.

ROW 17: Switch colors (knit with B, purl with A) and work in established patt.

ROWS 18–20: Change back to original colors and work 3 rows in patt.

ROW 21: Switch colors (knit with B, purl with A) and work in established patt.

ROW 22: Change back to original colors and work 1 row in patt.

ROW 23: Work Tk3tog (2 sl sts tog with 1 fan st after them), work to end of chart, knit 2 selvedge sts—574 sts total: 2 selvedge sts, [50 fan sts, 2 foundation] 10 times, 50 fan sts, 2 selvedge sts.

Using B for the knits and A for the purls, use the decrease ribbed-chain bind-off method (see page 31) to BO all sts.

Finishing

Weave in loose ends separately and as invisibly as possible (see page 45).

Mothwing
SCARF

Like the wings on a moth, this scarf is narrow in the center and flares into dramatic triangular ends that drape beautifully in soft folds, showing off the lacy leaf pattern. The narrow center section divides into two mirror-image "wings" and finishes with a delicate feathered edging. I used laceweight yarn for the light scarf shown here, giving it a beautiful drape; try a sportweight yarn (and larger needles) for a heavier version.

FINISHED SIZE
About 1½" (3.8 cm) wide in center, 17" (43 cm) wide at each end, and 51" (129.5 cm) long.

Yarn
Laceweight (#0 Lace).

Shown here: Malabrigo Silkpaca (70% baby alpaca, 30% silk; 420 yd [385 m]/50 g): #9 Polar Morn (light; A) and #52 Paris Night (dark; B), 1 skein each.

Note: One scarf requires about 370 yd (338 m) of each color.

Needles
Size U.S. 2 (2.75 mm).

Adjust needle size if necessary to obtain the correct gauge.

Notions
Size D/3 or E/4 (3.25 or 3.5 mm) crochet hook and smooth cotton waste yarn for provisional cast-on; stitch holder; sharp-point tapestry needle.

Gauge
47 sts and 32 rows = 4" (10 cm) in Twigg stitch patt from First and Second Wing charts.

Techniques

- ○ Basic Twigg stitch, page 10.
- ○ Italian cast-on, page 22.
- ○ Vicki's single-color ribbed bind-off, page 26.

Stitch Guide

Tk: Twigg-knit so that the knit yarn traps the purl yarn.

Tp: Twigg-purl so that the purl yarn traps the knit yarn.

Tk2tog: Twigg-knit 2 sts tog (1 of each color) using the knit yarn.

Tp2tog: Twigg-purl 2 sts tog (1 of each color) using the purl yarn.

Tk3tog: Twigg-knit 3 sts tog (2 knit stitches plus the purl stitch between them) using the knit yarn.

Tp3tog: Twigg-purl 3 sts tog (2 purl stitches plus the knit stitch between them) using the purl yarn.

Tkf&b: Twigg-knit into front and back of next st using the knit yarn.

Tpb&f: Twigg-purl into back and front of next st using the purl yarn.

ryo: (reverse yarnover) Bring both yarns from back to front over the top of the right needle tip and between the two needles to the back again to create a double-strand loop with a reverse mount. On the following row, work Tk1, Tp1 into the back of the double-strand loop—2 sts made from 2-strand ryo (see page 37).

NOTES

Knit with A and purl with B on all odd-numbered rows. Knit with B and purl with A on all even-numbered rows. ● For a tidy selvedge, bring the knit yarn over the top of the purl yarn at the beginning of every row (see page 40). ● The instructions include an option for adjusting the scarf length; if making a longer scarf, you'll need more yarn. ● The first time you work each wing chart there will only be enough stitches to work the red-outlined pattern repeat box once. Each time you work Rows 25–44 again, enough stitches will have been added to work one additional 20-stitch repeat. For example, after finishing Row 44 the first time, there will be 48 stitches, which is enough to work the 20-stitch repeat twice when the pattern starts over again at Row 25. After completing Row 44 the second time, there will be 68 stitches, which is enough to work the 20-stitch repeat three times when the pattern begins again, and so on.

Scarf

Using the Italian CO method (see page 22), make a crochet chain about 15 sts long and place 10 sts on the left needle. Make a slipknot with yarns A and B held tog and place on the right needle. The slipknot will secure the yarns for the first row of knitting; it does not count as a stitch.

Center Section

ROW 1: [Tk1, Tp1] 5 times (see Notes).

ROW 2: [Tk1, Tp1] 5 times. Drop the slipknot.

ROW 3: [Tk1, Tp1] 2 times, ryo (see Stitch Guide), Tk1, Tp1, ryo, [Tk1, Tp1] 2 times—14 sts; counting each ryo as 2 sts on this and all foll rows.

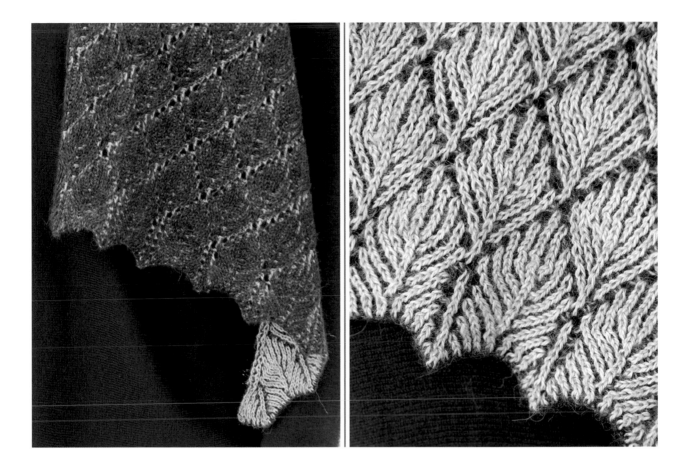

EVEN-NUMBERED ROWS 4–12: Work even in established patt, working [Tk1 with B, Tp1 with A] into double strand of each ryo.

ROW 5: [Tk1, Tp1] 2 times, ryo, [Tk1, Tp1, ryo] 3 times, [Tk1, Tp1] 2 times—22 sts.

ROW 7: [Tk1, Tp1] 2 times, ryo, work 6 sts as established, ryo, Tk1, Tp1, ryo, work 6 sts as established, ryo, [Tk1, Tp1] 2 times—30 sts.

ROW 9: [Tk1, Tp1] 2 times, ryo, work 10 sts as established, ryo, Tk1, Tp1, ryo, work 10 sts as established, ryo, [Tk1, Tp1] 2 times—38 sts.

ROW 11: [Tk1, Tp1] 2 times, ryo, work 14 sts as established, ryo, Tk1, Tp1, ryo, work 14 sts as established, ryo, [Tk1, Tp1] 2 times—46 sts.

ROW 13: [Tk1, Tp1] 2 times, ryo, work 18 sts as established, ryo, work Tkf&b (see Stitch Guide) into next st with A, Tpb&f (see Stitch Guide) into next st with B, ryo,

work 18 sts as established, ryo, [Tk1, Tp1] 2 times—56 sts; the f&b incs will create 2 A sts next to each other and 2 B sts next to each other in the center of the row.

ROW 14: Work 27 sts as established, switch the next 2 sts on the needle, bringing the knit st in front of the purl st as you cross them to make an even rib, then work as established to end of row.

First Wing

Establish patt from First Wing chart (see page 94) as foll:

ROW 15: (A side; Row 15 of chart) [Tk1, Tp1] 2 times, ryo, Tk1, Tp1, ryo, work 6 sts as established, Tk3tog (see Stitch Guide), Tp3tog (see Stitch Guide), work 10 sts as established, place rem 28 sts onto holder for second wing—28 sts rem.

Turn, and cont with Row 16 of chart. Work to Row 44 of chart once—48 sts. Work Rows 25–44 seven more times

FIRST WING

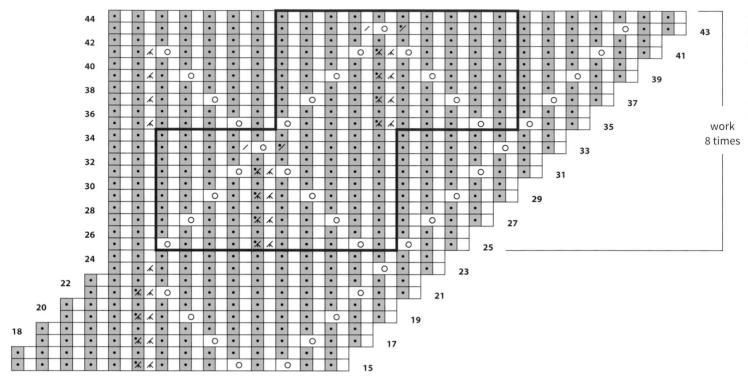

20-st repeat in Rows 25 to 44
See Notes.

FIRST EDGING

20-st repeat, inc'd to 22-st repeat in Row 9

SECOND EDGING

20-st repeat, inc'd to 22-st repeat in Row 9

SECOND WING

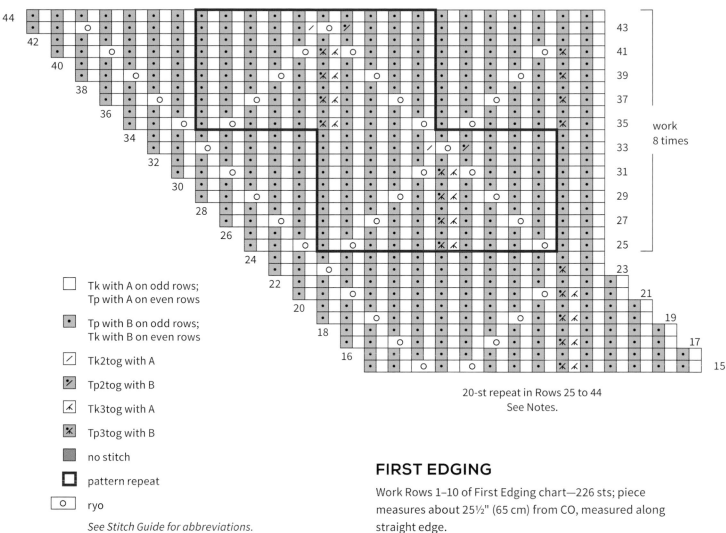

work
8 times

20-st repeat in Rows 25 to 44
See Notes.

☐ Tk with A on odd rows;
Tp with A on even rows

▪ Tp with B on odd rows;
Tk with B on even rows

╱ Tk2tog with A

╲ Tp2tog with B

⟋ Tk3tog with A

▨ Tp3tog with B

▨ no stitch

☐ pattern repeat

○ ryo

See Stitch Guide for abbreviations.

(see Notes), then work Rows 25–34 once more—198 sts; 194 rows total, including center section; piece measures about 24¼" (61.5 cm) from CO, measured along straighter edge at end of A (light)-side rows.

note: To adjust the scarf length, rep Rows 25–44 more or fewer times before working the final ten rows to end with Row 34; every twenty-row repeat added or removed will increase or decrease the length of each half by about 2½" (6.5 cm) and the total length of the scarf by about 5" (12.5 cm).

FIRST EDGING

Work Rows 1–10 of First Edging chart—226 sts; piece measures about 25½" (65 cm) from CO, measured along straight edge.

With B, use Vicki's single-color ribbed method (see page 26) starting with the ssk to BO all sts.

Second Wing

With A side facing, return 28 held sts to left needle. Make a slipknot of both yarns held tog and place on right needle tip to secure the yarns (drop this slipknot after Row 16).

Establish patt from Second Wing chart as foll:

ROW 15: (A side; Row 15 of chart) [Tk1, Tp1] 5 times, Tk3tog, Tp3tog, work 6 sts as established, ryo, Tk1, Tp1, ryo, [Tk1, Tp1] 2 times—28 sts.

Turn and cont with Row 16 of chart. Work to Row 44 of chart—48 sts. Work Rows 25–44 seven more times (or same number of reps as first wing if you changed the length), then work Rows 25–34 once more—198 sts; 194 rows total, including center section; piece measures about 24¼" (61.5 cm) from CO, measured along straighter edge at beg of A (light)-side rows.

EDGING

Work Rows 1–10 of Second Edging chart—226 sts; piece measures about 25½" (65 cm) from CO, measured along straight edge.

With B, use Vicki's ribbed method starting with the ssk to BO all sts.

Finishing

Carefully remove waste yarn from CO (the edge will not ravel). Bring the beginning and end of the CO sts together and use the yarns separately on each side to sew across the join, disguising the seam so the edging looks continuous.

Weave in loose ends separately and as invisibly as possible (see page 45).

Double Diamond
BEANIE

This close-fitting Twigg-stitch beanie is worked in rounds from the cast-on at the crown to the bind-off at the brim. The top shaping is worked outward from the center in eight increasing sections, then the stitch count remains constant for the color-switch diamond pattern. The design is completely reversible and a whole lot easier to knit than it looks—it's sure to turn a lot of heads!

FINISHED SIZE

About 11½ (13½, 15¼, 17¼, 19)" (29 [34.5, 38.5, 44, 48.5] cm) head circumference unstretched and 4½ (5¼, 6¼, 7, 7¾)" (11.5 [13.5, 16, 18, 19.5] cm) tall; will stretch to accommodate heads about 14½ (17, 19¼, 21¾, 24)" (37 [43, 49, 55, 61] cm) in circumference.

Shown in size 19" (48.5 cm).

Yarn

Sportweight (#2 Fine).

Shown here: Brown Sheep Lamb's Pride Superwash Sport (100% superwash wool; 180 yd [165 m]/50 g): #SW81 Red Baron (A) and #SW04 Charcoal Heather (B), 1 skein each for all sizes.

Note: Hat shown, which is in largest size, required about 103 yd (94 m) of each color.

Needles

Size U.S. 4 (3.5 mm): set of 5 double-pointed (dpn).

Adjust needle size if necessary to obtain the correct gauge.

Notions

Marker; sharp-point tapestry needle.

Gauge

33½ sts and 28 rnds = 4" (10 cm) in Twigg stitch, worked in rnds.

Techniques

- ○ Basic Twigg stitch, page 10.
- ○ Twigg-stitch color-switch, page 42.
- ○ Slimline-rib bind-off, page 33.

Stitch Guide

Tk: Twigg-knit so that the knit yarn traps the purl yarn.

Tp: Twigg-purl so that the purl yarn traps the knit yarn.

Tk3tog: Twigg-knit 3 sts tog (2 knit stitches plus the purl stitch between them) using the knit yarn.

Tp3tog: Twigg-purl 3 sts tog (2 purl stitches plus the knit stitch between them) using the purl yarn.

Ldec: Tk1, then Tp3tog—4 sts dec'd to 2 sts; 2 sts of each color dec'd to 1 st of each color.

Rdec: Tk3tog, then Tp1—4 sts dec'd to 2 sts; 2 sts of each color dec'd to 1 st of each color.

ryo: (reverse yarnover) Bring both yarns from back to front over the top of the right needle tip and between the two needles to the back again to create a double-strand loop with a reverse mount. On the following row, work Tk1, Tp1 into the back of the double-strand loop—2 sts made from 2-strand ryo (see page 37).

CHANGING COLORS FOR COLOR-SWITCH DIAMOND PATTERN

Most of the Double Diamond Beanie is worked using color A for the Twigg-knit stitches and color B for the Twigg-purl stitches. The set of diamonds around the middle of the hat is worked in a color-switch pattern in which B is used for the knit stitches and A is used for the purl stitches. To keep the fabric balanced, handle the yarns at the color changes as follows:

ODD-NUMBERED ROUNDS

Switch B to knit and A to purl: Exchange the position of the two yarns in your hand(s) by adding an extra twist, then work the indicated stitches (always an even number) using B to knit and A to purl, maintaining the rib as established.

To switch the colors back to original positions: Exchange the two yarns the other way to take out the twist, then continue with the original colors.

EVEN-NUMBERED ROUNDS

Switch B to knit and A to purl: Exchange the position of the two yarns in your hand(s) by taking out the twist, then work the indicated stitches (always an even number) using B to knit and A to purl, maintaining the rib as established.

To switch the colors back to original positions: Exchange the two yarns the other way to add an extra twist, then continue with the original colors.

Beanie

Holding both yarns tog, make a slipknot and place it on a needle held in your left hand, then use the e-wrap method (see page 14) to make a loop of both yarns next to the slipknot. Without removing the e-wrap loop from the needle and using A for the knit sts and B for the purl sts, *work [Tk1, Tp1] 4 times into the e-wrap loop; use another needle to rep from *, then slip the e-wrap loop from the left needle—16 sts total; 8 sts on each needle. Drop the slipknot from the needle. Do not turn work.

Shape Crown

notes: Throughout the crown shaping, always knit with A and purl with B and work two stitches into the double strand of each ryo by working [Tk1 with A, Tp1 with with B]. The photos above show the crown with the opposite side (knit with B; purl with A) worn on the outside.

RND 1: *Tk1, Tp1; rep from *.

RND 2: *Tk1, Tp1, ryo (see Stitch Guide); rep from *, beginning a new needle after every 2 reps and taking care not to drop any ryo that occurs at the end of a needle.

RND 3: *Tk1, Tp1, work 2 sts in ryo; rep from *—32 sts total; 8 sts each on 4 needles.

Work Tk1, Tp1, place marker (pm) for beg of rnd—rnd now begins after the first 2 sts of first dpn.

RND 4: *Ryo, work 4 sts as established; rep from * 7 more times to end at m.

RND 5: *Work 2 sts in ryo, work 4 sts as established; rep from *—48 sts; 12 sts each needle.

RND 6: *Ryo, work 6 sts as established; rep from *.

RND 7: *Work 2 sts in ryo, work 6 sts as established, rep from *—64 sts; 16 sts each needle.

RND 8: *Ryo, work 8 sts as established; rep from *.

RND 9: *Work 2 sts in ryo, work 8 sts as established, rep from *—80 sts; 20 sts each needle.

Cont in this manner, work 1 (3, 5, 7, 9) more rnd(s), working a ryo to inc 2 sts in each section on the even-numbered rnd(s), and ending with an even-numbered rnd—96 (112, 128, 144, 160) sts, counting each ryo as 2 sts; 24 (28, 32, 36, 40) sts each needle; 10 (12, 14, 16, 18) sts between ryos; piece measures about 1½ (1¾, 2, 2¼, 2½)" (3.8 [4.5, 5, 5.5, 6.5] cm) from CO.

First Half of Color-Switch Diamond Pattern

In this section, the first set of main-color diamonds are completed by decreasing them to points while new color-switch diamonds are worked in between them, starting with the 2 stitches worked into each ryo. Add or remove twist between the yarns as described in Changing Colors for Color-Switch Diamond Pattern on page 100.

RND 1: *Work 2 color-switch sts in ryo, exchange colors, then work 10 (12, 14, 16, 18) sts as established, rep from *—8 sections with 12 (14, 16, 18, 20) sts each; 2 color-switch diamond sts at beg of each section.

Remove m, work 2 diamond sts in color-switch, replace m to designate new beg of rnd—rnd now begins after the first 4 sts on first dpn; each section now ends with 2 color-switch diamond sts.

RND 2: *Work 8 (10, 12, 14, 16) sts as established to 2 sts before first color-switch st, work color-switch Rdec (next 2 sts tog with 2 color-switch sts after them; see Stitch Guide), ryo; rep from *.

RND 3: *Work 8 (10, 12, 14, 16) sts as established, work 2 color-switch sts, [Tk1 with B, Tp1 with A] in double strand of ryo; rep from *.

RND 4: *Work 6 (8, 10, 12, 14) sts as established, work color-switch Rdec, work 2 color-switch sts, ryo; rep from *.

RND 5: *Work 6 (8, 10, 12, 14) sts as established, work 4 color-switch sts, [Tk1 with B, Tp1 with A] in double strand of ryo; rep from *.

RND 6: *Work 4 (6, 8, 10, 12) sts as established, work color-switch Rdec, work 4 color-switch sts, ryo; rep from *.

RND 7: *Work 4 (6, 8, 10, 12) sts as established, work 6 color-switch sts, [Tk1 with B, Tp1 with A] in double strand of ryo; rep from *.

Work 2 (4, 6, 8, 10) more rnds this manner to end with an odd-numbered rnd, working 2 fewer main patt sts before the dec and 2 more diamond sts between the dec and the ryo in each even-numbered rnd—2 main-color sts and 10 (12, 14, 16, 18) color-switch diamond sts rem in each section.

NEXT RND: *Work color-switch Rdec, work 8 (10, 12, 14, 16) color-switch sts as established, ryo; rep from *—no main-color sts rem.

Second Half of Color-Switch Diamond Pattern

In this section, the color-switch diamonds are completed by decreasing them to points, and new diamonds are worked in between them using the original colors, starting with the 2 stitches worked into each ryo. Continue to add or remove twist when exchanging colors as before.

RND 1: *Work 10 (12, 14, 16, 18) color-switch sts, [Tk1 with A, Tp1 with B] in ryo; rep from * 6 more times, work 10 (12, 14, 16, 18) color-switch sts, ending without working last ryo of rnd.

Temporarily slip double strand of ryo to right needle, remove beg-of-rnd m, return slipped ryo strands to left needle correcting the mount so the leading leg is at the front, and replace m to designate new beg of rnd before the unworked ryo.

RND 2: Work a new ryo, Tk1 with A in double strand of ryo without dropping it from the left needle, Tp3tog (see Stitch Guide) with B in double strand of ryo and the next 2 sts after it, work 8 (10, 12, 14, 16) sts in color-switch, *ryo, work main-color Ldec (2 sts in original colors with 2 color-switch sts after them; see Stitch Guide), work 8 (10, 12, 14, 16) color-switch sts; rep from *.

RND 3: *[Tk1 with A, Tp1 with B] in double strand of ryo, work 2 sts as established, work 8 (10, 12, 14, 16) sts in color-switch; rep from *.

RND 4: *Ryo, work 2 sts as established, work main-color Ldec, work 6 (8, 10, 12, 14) sts in color-switch; rep from *.

RND 5: *[Tk1 with A, Tp1 with B] in double strand of ryo, work 4 sts as established, work 6 (8, 10, 12, 14) sts in color-switch, rep from *.

RND 6: *Ryo, work 4 sts as established, work main-color Ldec, work 4 (6, 8, 10, 12) sts in color-switch; rep from *.

RND 7: *[Tk1 with A, Tp1 with B] in double strand of ryo, work 6 sts as established, work 4 (6, 8, 10, 12) sts in color-switch, rep from *.

RND 8: *Ryo, work 6 sts as established, work main-color Ldec, work 2 (4, 6, 8, 10) sts in color-switch; rep from *.

Work 1 (3, 5, 7, 9) more rnd(s) in this manner to end with an odd-numbered rnd, working 2 more main-color sts between the ryo and the dec, and working 2 fewer color-switch diamond sts in each even-numbered rnd—10 (12, 14, 16, 18) main-color sts and 2 color-switch diamond sts rem in each section.

NEXT RND: *Ryo, work 8 (10, 12, 14, 16) main-color sts, work main-color Ldec; rep from *—no color-switch sts rem.

NEXT RND: Work as established, working [Tk1 with A, Tp1 with B] in double strand of each ryo—piece measures about 4½ (5¼, 6¼, 7, 7¾)" (11.5 [13.5, 16, 18, 19.5] cm) from CO.

> note: For a cuffed-brim–style hat, continue even in established patt for desired length.

Change colors so that A is in the purl position and B is in the knit position and use the slimline method (see page 33) to BO all sts. (For an alternate finish, use a single color and Vicki's ribbed BO method as described on page 26.)

Finishing

Untie the slipknot at the beg of the CO, pull the starting tails to close the hole in the center of the CO, then thread each tail one at a time on a chenille needle and secure as invisibly as possible.

Weave in loose ends separately and as invisibly as possible (see page 45), using the ending tails to sew a few sts across the gap between the first and last BO sts to disguise the join and create a seamless appearance around the BO edge.

Snowflake
EARFLAP HAT

This thick and cozy hat features a snowflake pattern, earflaps, and braided ties. It begins with a two-color braided-cable cast-on for a decorative edge, then the earflaps are worked one at a time in short-rows. The snowflake design is worked using the color-switch technique, in which the knit and purl yarns change position, then the hat is topped off with a distinctive decrease pattern. Weave in the ends carefully for a totally reversible hat!

FINISHED SIZE
About 19¾" (50 cm) head circumference, unstretched, and 8¼" (21 cm) tall, excluding earflaps; will stretch to accommodate heads up to 22" (56 cm).

Yarn
Worsted weight (#4 Medium).

Shown here: Malabrigo Rios (100% superwash merino; 210 yd [192 m]/100 g): #63 Natural (A) and #150 Azul Profundo (B), 1 skein each.

Note: One hat requires about 105 yd (96 m) of each color.

Needles
Hat: size U.S. 5 (3.75 mm): set of 5 double-pointed (dpn).

Cast-On: size U.S. 7 (4.5 mm): straight or circular (cir) needle in any length.

Adjust needle size if necessary to obtain the correct gauge.

Notions
4 markers (m); sharp-point tapestry needle; size F/5 (3.75 mm) crochet hook (used to attach braids; exact size is not important).

Gauge
26 sts and 24 rnds = 4" (10 cm) in Twigg stitch, worked in rnds on smaller needles.

Techniques

- Basic Twigg stitch, page 10.
- Braided-cable cast-on, page 19.
- Twigg-stitch color-switch stitch, page 42.

Stitch Guide

Tk: Twigg-knit so that the knit yarn traps the purl yarn.

Tp: Twigg-purl so that the purl yarn traps the knit yarn.

Tk2tog: Twigg-knit 2 stitches together (1 of each color) using the knit yarn.

Tp2tog: Twigg-purl 2 stitches together (1 of each color) using the purl yarn.

Tk3tog: Twigg-knit 3 stitches together (2 knit stitches plus the purl stitch between them) using the knit yarn.

Tp3tog: Twigg-purl 3 stitches together (2 purl stitches plus the knit stitch between them) using the purl yarn.

2 lifted sts: Insert right needle tip into the knit stitch below the next stitch on the needle from back to front and lift it (without the purl yarn carried across it) onto the left needle tip, then Tk the lifted loop and next stitch together. Slip the next purl stitch, insert the left needle tip into the purl stitch below the stitch on the right needle from front to back and lift it (without the knit yarn carried across it) onto the right needle tip, slip the lifted loop and stitch after it back onto the left needle and Tp them together—2 sts incorporated from side of earflap.

CHANGING COLORS IN TWIGG STITCH COLOR-SWITCH

The background of this hat is worked with color A for the Twigg-knit stitches and color B for the Twigg-purl stitches. To create the pattern, the colors are temporarily exchanged so that B is used for the knit stitches and A is used for the purl stitches. After working the pattern stitches, the colors switch back to their original assignments: A for knit stitches and B for purl stitches. To keep the fabric balanced, handle the yarns at the color changes as follows:

ODD-NUMBERED ROUNDS

Switch B to knit and A to purl: Exchange the position of the two yarns in your hand(s), adding an extra twist, then work the marked stitches (always an even number) using B to knit and A to purl, maintaining the rib as established.

To switch the colors back to original positions: Exchange the two yarns the other way to take out the twist, then continue with the original colors.

EVEN-NUMBERED ROUNDS

Switch B to knit and A to purl: Exchange the position of the two yarns in your hand(s) by taking out the twist, then work the marked stitches (always an even number) using B to knit and A to purl, maintaining the rib as established.

To switch the colors back to original positions: Exchange the two yarns the other way to add an extra twist, then continue with the original colors.

NOTE

If you would like to omit the earflaps, cast on as specified using the larger needles, omit the short-row instructions for the earflaps, change to the smaller needles and work 1 row in Tk1, Tp1 rib, then skip directly to the directions for the body.

Hat

With larger needle(s), use the braided-cable method (see page 19) to CO 128 sts, beginning with an e-wrap stitch in B.

Earflaps

> note: For tidy selvedges on the short-rows, bring the knit yarn over the purl yarn when changing the colors at the beginning of each row (see page 40).

Transfer the CO sts onto smaller needles, placing markers (pm) as foll: 10 sts for half of back-of-head sts, pm, 34 sts for left earflap, pm, 38 sts for front-of-head, pm, 34 sts for right earflap, pm, and 12 sts for other half of back-of-head. Do not join for working in rnds yet.

Work Twigg stitch in short-rows as foll:

ROW 1: (knit with A; purl with B) [Tk1, Tp1] 5 times to first m, slip marker (sl m) [Tk1, Tp1] 9 times, turn work.

ROW 2: (knit with B; purl with A) Tk1, Tp1, turn work—16 unworked sts rem at each side of 34-st earflap section.

ROW 3: (knit with A; purl with B) [Tk1, Tp1] 2 times, turn work.

ROW 4: (knit with B; purl with A) [Tk1, Tp1] 2 times, work 2 lifted sts (see Stitch Guide), turn work—14 un-worked earflap sts rem at each side.

ROW 5: (knit with A; purl with B) [Tk1, Tp1] 4 times, turn work.

ROW 6: (knit with B; purl with A) [Tk1, Tp1] 4 times, work 2 lifted sts, turn work—12 unworked earflap sts rem at each side.

Cont in this manner for 12 more rows to end with an even-numbered row, working 2 sts past the previous turning point at the end of each odd-numbered row, and working 2 lifted sts at the end of each even-numbered row—all 34 earflap sts have been worked.

NEXT ROW: (knit with A; purl with B) Work 34 left earflap sts as established, sl m, work 38 front-of-head sts as [Tk1, Tp1] 19 times to the third m, sl m, [Tk1, Tp1] 9 times for right earflap, turn work.

Beg with Row 2, work 34 right earflap sts as for left earflap, ending with an even-numbered row.

NEXT ROW: (knit with A; purl with B) Work 34 right earflap sts as established, sl m, work rem 12 sts for half of back-of-head as [Tk1, Tp1] 6 times, do not turn work.

Body

The body of the hat is worked in the round with the predominantly A side (knit with A; purl with B) facing outwards. Join for working in rnds. Remove old markers as you come to them in the first chart rnd.

Work patt from Snowflake chart (see page 109) as foll:

RND 1: Exchanging colors as described on page 106 for odd-numbered rnds, *work 14 sts as established, 2 color-switch sts (knit with B; purl with A), 16 sts as established, place new m at end of chart patt; rep from * 3 more times.

RND 2: Exchanging colors as described on page 106 for even-numbered rnds, work as for Rnd 1.

RNDS 3–34: Exchanging yarns for color-switch sts as established, work Rnds 3–34 of chart—piece measures about 5¾" (14.5 cm) from CO at center front or back (not including earflaps).

Shape Crown

Remove end-of-rnd m, work 14 sts in established patt (knit with A; purl with B), pm for new beg of rnd. Remove rem markers between reps of chart patt as you come to them in the first crown rnd.

Cont to knit with A and purl with B, shape crown as foll:

RND 1: *Work 12 sts as established, Tk3tog (see Stitch Guide), Tp1, work 2 sts as established, Tk1, Tp3tog (see

Stitch Guide), work 10 sts as established; rep from * 3 more times—112 sts rem.

EVEN-NUMBERED RNDS 2–10: Work even in patt as established.

RND 3: *Work 10 sts as established, Tk3tog, Tp1, work 2 sts as established, Tk1, Tp3tog, work 8 sts as established; rep from * 3 more times—96 sts rem.

RND 5: *Work 8 sts as established, Tk3tog, Tp1, work 2 sts as established, Tk1, Tp3tog, work 6 sts as established; rep from * 3 more times—80 sts rem.

RND 7: *Work 6 sts as established, Tk3tog, Tp1, work 2 sts as established, Tk1, Tp3tog, work 4 sts as established; rep from * 3 more times—64 sts rem.

RND 9: *Work 4 sts as established, Tk3tog, Tp1, work 2 sts as established, Tk1, Tp3tog, work 2 sts as established; rep from * 3 more times—48 sts rem.

RND 11: *Work 2 sts as established, Tk3tog, Tp1, work 2 sts as established, Tk1, Tp3tog; rep from * 3 more times—32 sts rem.

RND 12: Work even as established to last st, temporarily sl last st to right needle, remove m, return last st to left needle, replace m—first st after m is now a purl st with B.

RND 13: [Tp2tog, Tk2tog] (see Stitch Guide) 8 times—16 sts rem.

RND 14: Beg with a purl st with B, work even as established—piece measures about 8¼" (21 cm) from CO at center front or back (not including earflaps).

Cut yarns, leaving 10" (25.5 cm) tails.

SNOWFLAKE

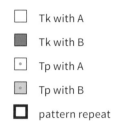

34
33
32
31
30
29
28
27
26
25
24
23
22
21
20
19
18
17
16
15
14
13
12
11
10
9
8
7
6
5
4
3
2
1

☐ Tk with A

■ Tk with B

☐ Tp with A

▨ Tp with B

☐ pattern repeat

32-st repeat

Thread A on a tapestry needle and draw through the A sts, thread B on a tapestry needle and draw through the B sts, remove the needles and tuck the B yarn and sts through to the other side, pull A tight to close hole, and secure as invisibly as possible. Turn hat inside out, pull B tight, and secure as for the A tail.

Finishing

Weave in loose ends separately and as invisibly as possible (see page 45), using the starting tails to disguise the gap between the first and last CO sts to create a seamless appearance along the CO edge.

Braids

Cut six 36" (91.5 cm) strands each of A and B. Use a crochet hook to thread 3 strands of A and 3 strands of B through the point at the bottom of an earflap, then pull the ends even to make 12 strands of equal length. Divide the 12 strands into 3 groups with 4 strands (2 A and 2 B) in each group and braid them. Firmly tie an overhand knot about 2" (5 cm) from the end of the strands and trim the loose ends below the knot even. Use the remaining 6strands to apply a second braid in the same manner to the other earflap.

4 STITCH DICTIONARY

This chapter is the result of many of my Twigg-stitch explorations. I applied Twigg stitch to as many different knitting techniques as I could think of and found it to work with most of them—from simple ribs (such as stripes, mistake-stitch surface patterns, and garter-stitch additions), to thinner fabrics with more drape (such as seed stitch, interrupted ribs, basketweave, and herringbone), to thicker fabrics (such as honeycomb). Twigg stitch also provides an excellent foundation for cables, textural patterns (some of which use more of one color than the other on each row), entrelac, lace, and colorwork. Finally, I offer some ideas for border and braid effects.

Many of these stitch patterns can be substituted for the patterns used in the projects in Chapter 3 or adapted for your own explorations. Whether you want to use them as allover patterns or as an accent or trim on an otherwise plain fabric, you'll find that Twigg stitch adds a reversible twist to many types of knitting.

Note that most of the instructions are for working back and forth in rows, not in rounds.

SYMBOL KEY FOR BASIC KNIT-PURL STITCH PATTERN CHARTS

- Tk with A on odd rows; Tp with A on even rows
- Tp with B on odd rows; Tk with B on even rows
- Tk with B on odd rows; Tp with B on even rows
- Tp with A on odd rows; Tk with A on even rows
- knit with A holding B in front on odd rows; purl with A holding B in back on even rows
- purl with B holding A in back on odd rows; knit with B holding A in front on even rows
- pattern repeat

 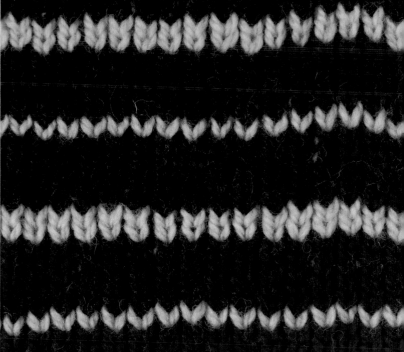

Basic Rib, front ◄ ▎ ► *Basic Rib, back*

Basic Knit-Purl Stitch Patterns

Because Twigg stitch is based on a knit-one-purl-one (k1, p1) rib, it's easily adapted for stitch patterns that alternate knit and purl stitches.

The swatches in this section demonstrate different ways in which basic Twigg stitch can produce exciting two-sided fabrics.

The swatches in this section were worked with Cascade Yarns 220 Sport (100 % wool; 164 yd [150 m]/50 g) in colors #9477 Tutu (pink; A) and #7803 Magenta (dark pink; B).

Basic Rib

This pattern is the foundation for most of the projects in this book—a simple alternation of Twigg knit and Twigg purl stitches. To create stripes, simply start the row with the colors the opposite way around for the knit and purl stitches. Stripe rows that appear light on one side will appear dark on the other and vice versa.

You can also add new colors by cutting the working yarn and joining a new color on one or both sides.

Basic Rib

ROW 1: (knit with A; purl with B) *Tk1, Tp1; rep from *.

ROW 2: (knit with B; purl with A) *Tk1, Tp1; rep from *.

Repeat Rows 1 and 2 for pattern.

BASIC RIB WITH STRIPES

This pattern creates two-row stripes. For different-width stripes, work as many rows as desired before switching the colors.

ROW 1: (knit with A; purl with B) *Tk1, Tp1; rep from *.

ROW 2: (knit with B; purl with A) *Tk1, Tp1; rep from *.

ROW 3: (knit with B; purl with A) *Tk1, Tp1; rep from *.

ROW 4: (knit with A; purl with B) *Tk1, Tp1; rep from *.

Repeat Rows 1–4 for pattern.

BASIC RIB

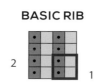

mult of 2 sts and 2 rows

BASIC RIB WITH STRIPES

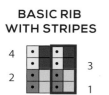

mult of 2 sts and 4 rows

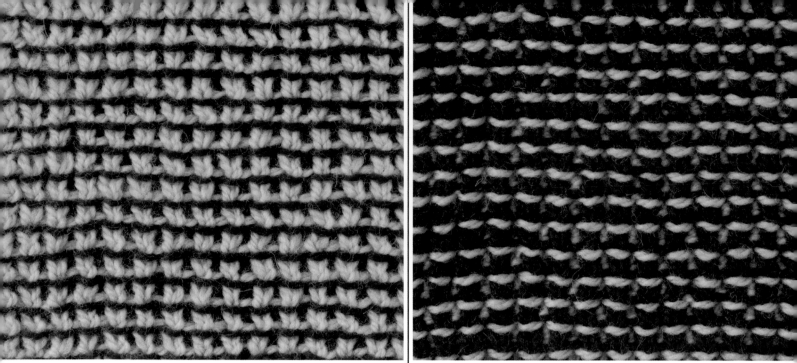

Allover Texture, front ◄ ► *Allover Texture, back*

Mistake Stitch

As you might guess, this pattern results from a simple mistake in the basic rib pattern. The "mistake" is made by leaving the purl yarn in the front while working a regular knit stitch or by leaving the knit yarn in the back while working a regular purl stitch. You can make the "mistake" on the knit stitches in every row to form an allover pattern or on selected stitches to form a wide range of graphic designs.

ALLOVER TEXTURE

In this variation, the purl yarn is held in front while each knit stitch is worked. You can get similar results by holding the knit yarn in back when working all the purl stitches. Because the knit and purl yarns switch every row, dark strands cross the light knit stitches on one side and light strands cross the dark knit stitches on the other. You'll get a traditional two-color rib if you work mistake purl stitches on odd-numbered rows and mistake knit stitches on even-numbered rows (or work mistake purl stitches all the time if working in rounds).

ROW 1: (knit with A; purl with B) *Holding B in front, mistake k1, bring both yarns to the front, Tp1; rep from *.

ROW 2: (knit with B; purl with A) *Holding A in front, mistake k1, bring both yarns to the front, Tp1; rep from *.

Repeat Rows 1 and 2 for pattern.

ALLOVER TEXTURE

2   1

mult of 2 sts and 2 rows
see page 110 for symbol key

MISTAKE-STITCH BRAID

In this variation, the purl yarn (dark) is held in front when selected knit stitches (light) are worked on odd-numbered rows and the knit yarn (dark) is held in back when selected purl stitches (light) are worked on even-numbered rows to form a graphic design on the front of the fabric. The reverse side of the fabric is solid (knit with dark; purl with light). This eighteen-row band can be used as a border or repeated as desired.

ROW 1: (knit with A; purl with B) *Tk1, Tp1; rep from *.

ROW 2: (knit with B; purl with A) *Tk1, hold B in back and p1, [Tk1, Tp1] 4 times, Tk1, hold B in back and p1; rep from *.

ROW 3: (knit with A; purl with B) *[Hold B in front and k1, Tp1] 2 times, [Tk1, Tp1] 2 times, [hold B in front and k1, Tp1] 2 times; rep from *.

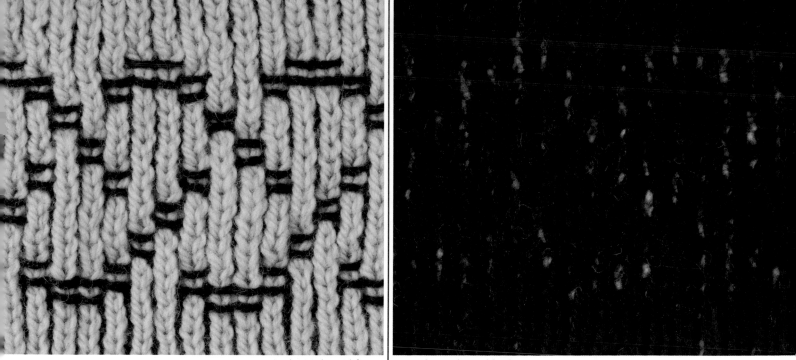

Mistake-Stitch Braid, front ◄ | ► Mistake-Stitch Braid, back

MISTAKE-STITCH BRAID

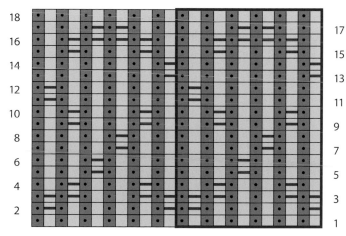

mult of 12 sts worked over 18 rows
see page 110 for symbol key

ROW 4: (knit with B; purl with A) *Tk1, Tp1, Tk1, hold B in back and p1, [Tk1, Tp1] 2 times, Tk1, hold B in back and p1, Tk1, Tp1; rep from *.

ROW 5: (knit with A; purl with B) *[Tk1, Tp1] 3 times, hold B in front and k1, Tp1, [Tk1, Tp1] 2 times; rep from *.

ROW 6: (knit with B; purl with A) *[Tk1, Tp1] 2 times, Tk1, hold B in back and p1, [Tk1, Tp1] 3 times; rep from *.

ROW 7: (knit with A; purl with B) *[Tk1, Tp1] 2 times, hold B in front and k1, Tp1, [Tk1, Tp1] 3 times; rep from *.

ROW 8: (knit with B; purl with A) *[Tk1, Tp1] 3 times, Tk1, hold B in back and p1, [Tk1, Tp1] 2 times; rep from *.

ROW 9: (knit with A; purl with B) *Tk1, Tp1, hold B in front and k1, Tp1, Tk1, Tp1; rep from *.

ROW 10: (knit with B; purl with A) *Tk1, Tp1, Tk1, hold B in back and p1, Tk1, Tp1; rep from *.

ROW 11: (knit with A; purl with B) *[Tk1, Tp1] 5 times, hold B in front and k1, Tp1; rep from *.

ROW 12: (knit with B; purl with A) *Tk1, hold B in back and p1, [Tk1, Tp1] 5 times; rep from *.

ROW 13: (knit with A; purl with B) *Hold B in front and k1, Tp1, [Tk1, Tp1] 5 times; rep from *.

ROW 14: (knit with B; purl with A) *[Tk1, Tp1] 5 times, Tk1, hold B in back and p1; rep from *.

ROW 15: (knit with A; purl with B) *Tk1, Tp1, hold B in front and k1, Tp1, Tk1, Tp1; rep from *.

ROW 16: (knit with B; purl with A) *Tk1, Tp1, [Tk1, hold B in back and p1] 4 times, Tk1, Tp1; rep from *.

ROW 17: (knit with A; purl with B) *[Tk1, Tp1] 2 times, [hold B in front and k1, Tp1] 2 times, [Tk1, Tp1] 2 times; rep from *.

ROW 18: (knit with B; purl with A) *Tk1, Tp1; rep from *.

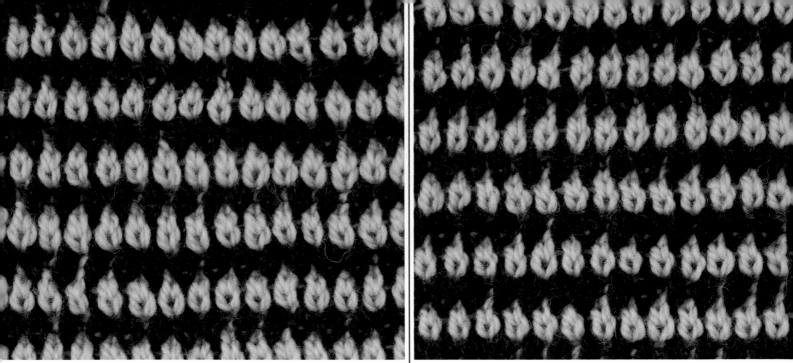

Horizontal Color Stripes, front ◄ | ► *Horizontal Color Stripes, back*

Interrupted Rib

You can get interesting patterns by switching the knit and purl stitches every few rows. In the following examples, a four-row pattern is worked two different ways. In the first, the same colors are used for each stitch, but the knits and purls are switched every two rows, resulting in equal amounts of light and dark yarns that form horizontal stripes on each side. In the second, the colors as well as the knits and purls are switched every two rows, resulting in a pebbly surface that is predominantly light on one side and predominantly dark on the other.

HORIZONTAL COLOR STRIPES

In this version, the stitch colors align vertically, but because the knits and purls are switched every 2 rows, the overall effect is one of horizontal stripes. Stripes that are light on one side appear dark on the other.

ROW 1: (knit with A; purl with B) *Tk1, Tp1; rep from *.

ROW 2: (knit with B; purl with A) *Tk1, Tp1; rep from *.

ROW 3: (knit with B; purl with A) *Tp1, Tk1; rep from *.

ROW 4: (knit with A; purl with B) *Tp1, Tk1; rep from *.

Repeat Rows 1–4 for pattern.

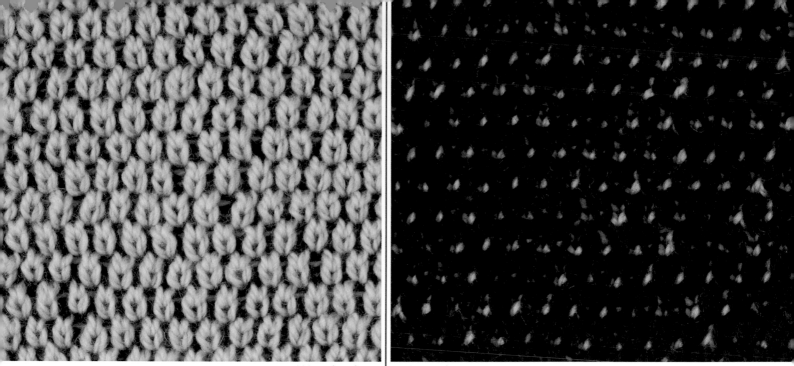

Pebbly Surface, front ◄ | ► *Pebbly Surface, back*

PEBBLY SURFACE

In this version, the colors as well as the knits and purls are switched every 2 rows to create a pebbly surface that is predominantly light on one side and predominantly dark on the other.

ROW 1: (knit with A; purl with B) *Tk1, Tp1; rep from *.

ROW 2: (knit with B; purl with A) *Tk1, Tp1; rep from *.

ROW 3: (knit with A; purl with B) *Tp1, Tk1; rep from *.

ROW 4: (knit with B; purl with A) *Tp1, Tk1; rep from *.

Repeat Rows 1–4 for pattern.

HORIZONTAL COLOR STRIPES

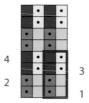

mult of 2 sts and 4 rows
see page 110 for symbol key

PEBBLY SURFACE

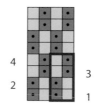

mult of 2 sts and 4 rows
see page 110 for symbol key

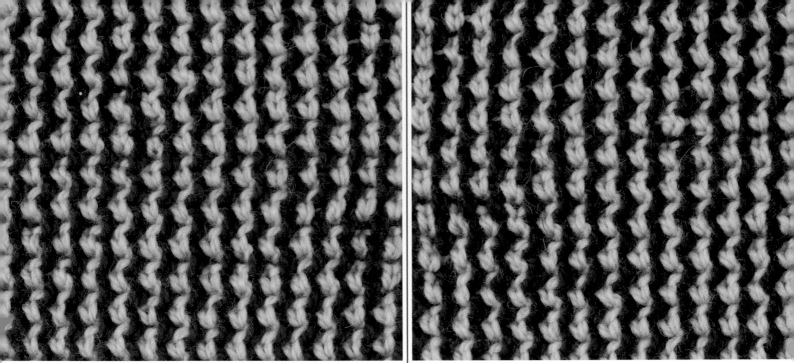

Vertical Color Stripes, front ◀ | ▶ *Vertical Color Stripes, back*

Seed Stitch

Seed stitch has an interesting effect when worked in Twigg stitch. You can work the colors to form vertical stripes, in which the two sides look the same, or you can produce a more mottled effect, in which one color dominates on one side and the other color dominates on the reverse.

VERTICAL COLOR STRIPES

In this variation, the same color is used to knit or purl each column of stitches throughout, but the placement of the knit and purl stitches is switched every row. The colors align vertically, and the two sides of the fabric look the same.

ROW 1: (knit with A; purl with B) *Tk1, Tp1; rep from *.

ROW 2: (knit with A; purl with B) *Tp1, Tk1; rep from *.

Repeat Rows 1 and 2 for pattern.

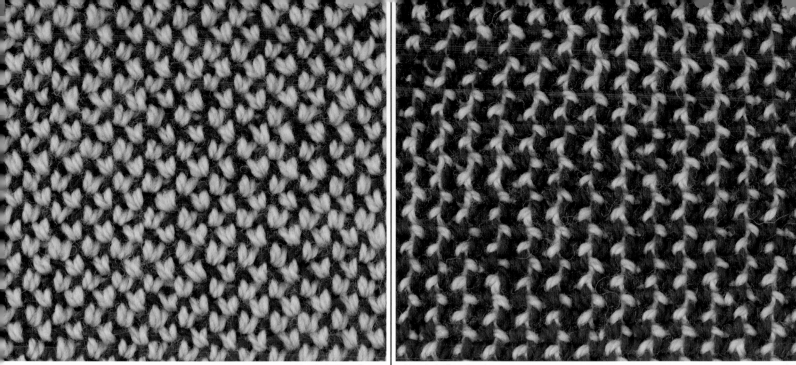

Mottled Effect, front ◄ | ► *Mottled Effect, back*

MOTTLED EFFECT

In this variation, the color positions as well as the knits and purls are switched every row to create a mottled effect. One side is predominantly light and the other is predominantly dark.

ROW 1: (knit with A; purl with B) *Tk1, Tp1; rep from *.

ROW 2: (knit with B; purl with A) *Tp1, Tk1; rep from *.

Repeat Rows 1 and 2 for pattern.

VERTICAL COLOR STRIPES

mult of 2 sts and 2 rows
see page 110 for symbol key

MOTTLED EFFECT

mult of 2 sts and 2 rows
see page 110 for symbol key

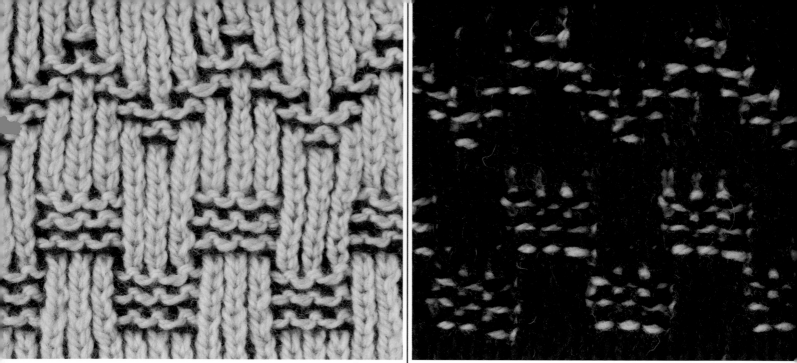

Subtle Effect, front ◀ | ▶ *Subtle Effect, back*

Garter-Stitch Designs

You can use garter stitch with Twigg stitch to form two-color patterns that look something like reversible stranded knitting. Matching the colors of the stitches in a basic Twigg-stitch background, the garter-stitch pattern is worked in pairs of rows that put garter ridges on both sides of the fabric. Depending on how you manipulate the two colors, you can create subtle or bold effects.

SUBTLE EFFECT

For this variation, hold the yarns the same way as for Twigg-stitch, but work the garter areas using all knit stitches, alternating the yarns to match the color of each existing stitch. The garter stitches are worked as regular knit stitches; do not twist the yarns around each other. One side will be predominantly light; the other will be predominantly dark. This twenty-six-row band can be used as a border.

ROW 1: (knit with A; purl with B) *K6 matching the st colors, [Tk1, Tp1] 3 times; rep from *.

ROW 2: (knit with B; purl with A) *[Tk1, Tp1] 3 times, k6 matching the st colors; rep from *.

ROWS 3–6: Rep Rows 1 and 2 two more times.

ROW 7: (knit with A; purl with B) *[Tk1, Tp1] 3 times, k6 matching the st colors; rep from *.

ROW 8: (knit with B; purl with A) *K6 matching the st colors, [Tk1, Tp1] 3 times; rep from *.

ROWS 9–12: Rep Rows 7 and 8 two more times.

ROWS 13 AND 15: (knit with A; purl with B) *Tk1, Tp1; rep from *.

ROWS 14 AND 16: (knit with B; purl with A) *Tk1, Tp1; rep from *.

ROW 17: (knit with A; purl with B) *Tk1, Tp1, k2 matching the st colors, [Tk1, Tp1] 4 times; rep from *.

ROW 18: (knit with B; purl with A) *[Tk1, Tp1] 4 times, k2 matching the st colors, Tk1, Tp1; rep from *.

ROW 19: (knit with A; purl with B) *K6 matching the st colors, [Tk1, Tp1] 3 times; rep from *.

ROW 20: (knit with B; purl with A) *[Tk1, Tp1] 3 times, k6 matching the st colors; rep from *.

ROW 21: (knit with A; purl with B) *K2 matching the st colors, Tk1, Tp1, k4 matching the st colors, Tk1, Tp1, k2 matching the st colors; rep from *.

ROW 22: (knit with B; purl with A) *K2 matching the st colors, Tk1, Tp1, k4 matching the st colors, Tk1, Tp1, k2 matching the st colors.

ROW 23: (knit with A; purl with B) *[Tk1, Tp1] 3 times, k6 matching the st colors; rep from *.

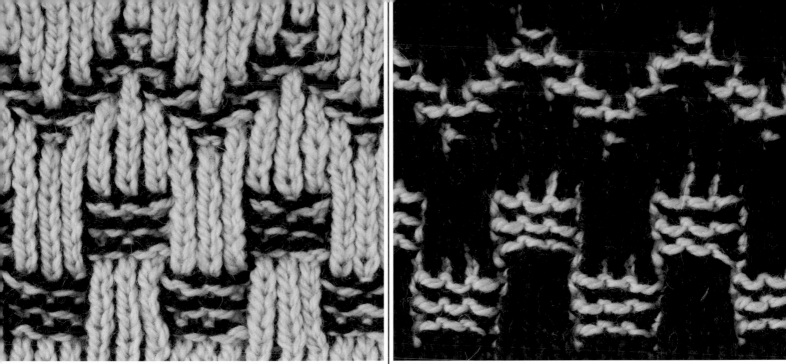

Bold Effect, front ◄ | ▶ Bold Effect, back

ROW 24: (knit with B; purl with A) *K6 matching the st colors, [Tk1, Tp1] 3 times; rep from *.

ROW 25: (knit with A; purl with B) *[Tk1, Tp1] 4 times, k2 matching the st colors, Tk1, Tp1; rep from *.

ROW 26: (knit with B; purl with A) *Tk1, Tp1, k2 matching the st colors, [Tk1, Tp1] 4 times; rep from *.

BOLD EFFECT

For this variation, switch the way you hold the yarns when working the regular knit stitches of the garter-stitch sections so that the opposite color becomes more dominant in the pattern. One side will be predominantly light; the other will be predominantly dark.

Follow the garter-stitch pattern or chart as for the subtle-effect swatch, but at the beginning of each garter-stitch section, switch the yarns in your hand(s) so that B is in the knit position and A is in the purl position (see page 42), creating an extra twist as you do so. Work the stitches of the garter-stitch section as regular knit stitches, alternating the yarns to match the color of each existing stitch. At the end of the garter-stitch section, switch the yarns back so that A is in the knit position and B is in the purl position, omitting the twist as you do so.

To work either of these patterns in the round, work the garter-stitch sections of the even-numbered rows by bringing both yarns to the front and purling the garter

GARTER-STITCH PATTERNING

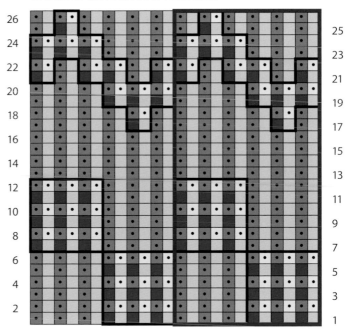

mult of 12 sts, worked over 26 rows
Work black-outlined garter sections as regular knit
sts on odd and even rows; see instructions.
see page 110 for symbol key

stitches with their matching stitch colors. Switch the yarns accordingly if you want the bolder effect.

Cable Patterns

Cables worked over an even number of stitches lend themselves well to Twigg-stitch patterns. This type of cable will be "balanced" and appear similar on the two sides of the fabric.

The swatches in this section were worked with Cascade Yarns 220 Sport (100% wool; 164 yd [150 m]/50 g) in #9594 Orchid Haze (light purple; A) and #2450 Mystic Purple (dark purple; B).

SYMBOL KEY FOR CABLE PATTERN CHARTS

☐	Tk with A on odd rows; Tp with A on even rows
⊡	Tp with B on odd rows; Tk with B on even rows
■	Tk with B on odd rows; Tp with B on even rows
⊡	Tp with A on odd rows; Tk with A on even rows
☐	pattern repeat
	2×2LC
	2×2RC
	4×4LC
	4×4RC
... or ...	C2kL with colors shown
... or ...	C2kR with colors shown
	CCL
	CCR

See below for cable definitions.

CABLE ABBREVIATIONS

cn: cable needle

2×2LC: (left-slant cable) Slip 2 sts onto a cn and hold in front of work, Tk1, Tp1, then Tk1, Tp1 from cn.

2×2RC: (right-slant cable) Slip 2 sts onto a cn and hold in back of work, Tk1, Tp1, then Tk1, Tp1 from cn.

4×4LC: (left-slant cable) Slip 4 sts onto a cn and hold in front of work, [Tk1, Tp1] 2 times, then [Tk1, Tp1] 2 times from cn.

4×4RC: (right-slant cable) Slip 4 sts onto a cn and hold in back of work, [Tk1, Tp1] 2 times, then [Tk1, Tp1] 2 times from cn.

C2kL: (cross 2 knit sts with left slant) Slip 1 knit st onto a cn and hold in front of the work, slip the next st (a purl st) onto a second cn and hold in back of the work, Tk1, then Tp1 from cn at back, then Tk1 from cn at front, then Tp1.

C2kR: (cross 2 knit sts with right slant) Slip 2 sts (one knit and one purl) onto a cn and hold in back of work, Tk1, slip the purl st from cn onto left needle tip, bring cn to front of work, Tp1, Tk1 from cn, then Tp1.

CCL: (crossover left-slant cable; forms right-slant cable on the other side) Slip the knit st onto a cn and hold in front of work, slip the purl st onto a second cn and hold in back of work, Tk1, Tp1, then Tk1 from front cn and Tp1 from back cn.

CCR: (crossover right-slant cable; forms left-slant cable on other side) Slip 2 sts (one knit and one purl) onto a cn and hold in back of work, Tk1, bring cn to the front of the work, Tp1, then slip the sts from the cn onto the left needle and work them as Tk1, Tp1.

 2×2LC and 2×2RC worked every two rows (left) and
2×2LC and 2×2RC worked every four rows (right), front

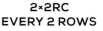 *2×2RC and 2×2LC worked every four rows (left) and*
2×2RC and 2×2LC worked every two rows (right), back

2×2 Cables

2×2 CABLE TWISTED EVERY TWO ROWS

SET-UP: Work Twigg stitch for 2 rows.

ROW 1: (knit with A; purl with B) Work 2×2LC or 2×2RC, depending on the desired direction of twist.

ROW 2: (knit with B; purl with A) Work even in rib as established.

Repeat Rows 1 and 2 for pattern.

2×2 CABLE TWISTED EVERY FOUR ROWS

SET-UP: Work Twigg st for 2 rows.

ROW 1: (knit with A; purl with B) Work 2×2LC or 2×2RC, depending on the desired direction of twist.

ROW 2: (knit with B; purl with A) Work even in rib as established.

ROW 3: (knit with A; purl with B) Work even in rib as established.

ROW 4: (knit with B; purl with A) Work even in rib as established.

Repeat Rows 1–4 for pattern.

2×2LC
EVERY 2 ROWS

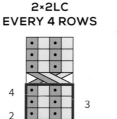

mult of 4 sts
and 2 rows
see page 120 for symbol key

2×2RC
EVERY 2 ROWS

mult of 4 sts
and 2 rows
see page 120 for symbol key

2×2LC
EVERY 4 ROWS

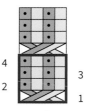

mult of 4 sts
and 4 rows
see page 120 for symbol key

2×2RC
EVERY 4 ROWS

mult of 4 sts
and 4 rows
see page 120 for symbol key

4×4LC worked every four rows (left), 4×4LC worked every six rows (center), 4×4LC worked every eight rows (right), front ◄

4×4 Cables

4×4 CABLE TWISTED EVERY FOUR ROWS

SET-UP: Work Twigg st for 2 rows.

ROW 1: (knit with A; purl with B) Work 4×4LC or 4×4RC, depending on the desired direction of twist.

ROW 2: (knit with B; purl with A) Work even in rib as established.

ROW 3: (knit with A; purl with B) Work even in rib as established.

ROW 4: (knit with B; purl with A) Work even in rib as established.

Repeat Rows 1–4 for pattern.

4×4 CABLE TWISTED EVERY SIX ROWS

SET-UP: Work Twigg st for 2 rows.

ROW 1: (knit with A; purl with B) Work 4×4LC or 4×4RC, depending on the desired direction of twist.

4×4LC EVERY 4 ROWS

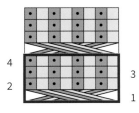

mult of 8 sts and 4 rows
see page 120 for symbol key

4×4RC EVERY 4 ROWS

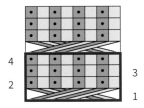

mult of 8 sts and 4 rows
see page 120 for symbol key

4×4LC EVERY 6 ROWS

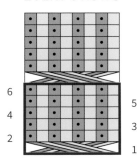

mult of 8 sts and 6 rows
see page 120 for symbol key

4×4RC EVERY 6 ROWS

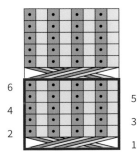

mult of 8 sts and 6 rows
see page 120 for symbol key

▶ *4×4LC worked every eight rows (left), 4×4LC worked every six rows (center), 4×4LC worked every four rows (right), back*

ROWS 2 AND 4: (knit with B; purl with A) Work even in rib as established.

ROWS 3 AND 5: (knit with A; purl with B) Work even in rib as established.

ROW 6: (knit with B; purl with A) Work even in rib as established.

Repeat Rows 1–6 for pattern.

4×4 CABLE TWISTED EVERY EIGHT ROWS

SET-UP: Work Twigg st for 2 rows.

ROW 1: (knit with A; purl with B) Work 4×4LC or 4×4RC, depending on the desired direction of twist.

ROWS 2, 4, AND 6: (knit with B; purl with A) Work even in rib as established.

ROWS 3, 5, AND 7: (knit with A; purl with B) Work even in rib as established.

ROW 8: (knit with B; purl with A) Work even in rib as established.

Repeat Rows 1–8 for pattern.

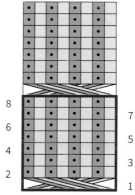

4×4LC EVERY 8 ROWS

mult of 8 sts and 8 rows
see page 120 for symbol key

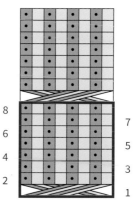

4×4RC EVERY 8 ROWS

mult of 8 sts and 8 rows
see page 120 for symbol key

Small braided cable (left); large braided cable (right), front ◀ | ▶ Large braided cable (left), small braided cable (right), dark

Braided Cables

Beautiful interlocking patterns occur when left- and right-twist cables are combined over a series of rows.

SMALL BRAIDED CABLE

SET-UP: Work Twigg st for 2 rows.

ROW 1: (knit with A; purl with B) 2x2RC, Tk1, Tp1.

ROW 2: (knit with B; purl with A) Work even in rib as established.

ROW 3: (knit with A; purl with B) Tk1, Tp1, 2x2LC.

ROW 4: (knit with B; purl with A) Work even in rib as established.

Repeat Rows 1–4 for pattern.

LARGE BRAIDED CABLE

SET-UP: Work Twigg st for 2 rows.

ROW 1: 4x4RC, [Tk1, Tp1] 2 times.

ROWS 2, 4, AND 6: (knit with B; purl with A) Work even in rib as established.

ROW 3: (knit with A; purl with B) Work even in rib as established.

ROW 5: [Tk1, Tp1] 2 times, 4x4LC.

ROW 7: (knit with A; purl with B) Work even in rib as established.

SMALL BRAIDED CABLE

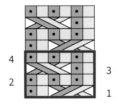

mult of 6 sts and 4 rows
see page 120 for symbol key

LARGE BRAIDED CABLE

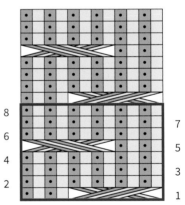

mult of 12 sts and 8 rows; see page 120 for symbol key

ROW 8: (knit with B; purl with A) Work even in rib as established.

Repeat Rows 1–8 for pattern.

One-Sided Traveling-Stitch Cables

It's quite possible to work traveling-stitch patterns on just one side of the fabric. In these examples, the pattern is worked every other row by switching the position of two knit stitches while leaving the purl stitches where they are.

The traveling-stitch braid (left) and diamonds (right), front ◄ | ► The traveling-stitch braid and diamond, back

TRAVELING-STITCH BRAID

SET-UP: Work Twigg st for 2 rows.

ROW 1: (knit with A; purl with B) C2kR, Tk1, Tp1.

ROW 2: (knit with B; purl with A) Work even in rib as established.

ROW 3: Tk1, Tp1, C2kL.

ROW 4: (knit with B; purl with A) Work even in rib as established.

Repeat Rows 1–4 for pattern.

TRAVELING-STITCH DIAMONDS

SET-UP: Work Twigg st for 2 rows.

ROW 1: (knit with A; purl with B) [Tk1, Tp1] 3 times, C2kR, [Tk1, Tp1] 3 times.

ROW 2 AND ALL EVEN-NUMBERED ROWS: (knit with B; purl with A) Work even in rib as established.

ROW 3: (knit with A; purl with B) [Tk1, Tp1] 2 times, C2kR, C2kL, [Tk1, Tp1] 2 times.

ROW 5: (knit with A; purl with B) Tk1, Tp1, C2kR, [Tk1, Tp1] 2 times, C2kL, Tk1, Tp1.

ROW 7: (knit with A; purl with B) C2kR, [Tk1, Tp1] 4 times, C2kL.

ROW 9: (knit with A; purl with B) C2kL, [Tk1, Tp1] 4 times, C2kR.

TRAVELING-STITCH BRAID

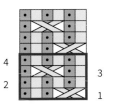

mult of 6 sts and 4 rows
see page 120 for symbol key

TRAVELING-STITCH DIAMONDS

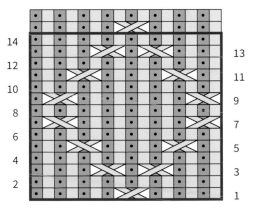

mult of 16 sts and 14 rows + 2; see page 120 for symbol key

ROW 11: (knit with A; purl with B) Tk1, Tp1, C2kL, [Tk1, Tp1] 2 times, C2kR, Tk1, Tp1.

ROW 13: (knit with A; purl with B) [Tk1, Tp1] 2 times, C2kL, C2kR, [Tk1, Tp1] 2 times.

ROW 14: (knit with B; purl with A) Work even in rib as established.

Repeat Rows 1–14 for pattern, then work Rows 1 and 2 once more to balance.

Traveling-Stitch Diamond Lattice and Wide Cable, front ◄ ► *Traveling-Stitch Diamond Lattice and Wide Cable, back*

Two-Sided Mismatched Traveling-Stitch Patterns

It's an easy transition to working a different one-sided cable pattern on each side of the fabric. In this case, a diamond lattice pattern is worked on the odd-numbered rows, and a wide pattern bordered with cables is worked on the even-numbered rows.

For clarity, the chart for each side of the fabric is shown as it appears, with no patterning given for the intervening rows. To knit the pattern, alternate rows from the two charts—work an odd-numbered row from Side 1 chart, then an even-numbered row from Side 2 chart.

TRAVELING-STITCH DIAMOND LATTICE AND WIDE CABLE

SET-UP: Work Twigg st for 2 rows.

ROW 1: (knit with A; purl with B) *[Tk1, Tp1] 3 times, C2kR, [Tk1, Tp1] 3 times; rep from * once.

ROW 2: (knit with B; purl with A) [Tk1, Tp1] 5 times, C2kL, [Tk1, Tp1] 2 times, C2kR, [Tk1, Tp1] 5 times.

ROW 3: (knit with A; purl with B) *[Tk1, Tp1] 2 times, C2kR, C2kL, [Tk1, Tp1] 2 times; rep from * once.

ROW 4: (knit with B; purl with A) C2kL, [Tk1, Tp1] 2 times, [C2kR] 2 times, [C2kL] 2 times, [Tk1, Tp1] 2 times, C2kR.

ROW 5: (knit with A; purl with B) *Tk1, Tp1, C2kR, [Tk1, Tp1] 2 times, C2kL, Tk1 Tp1; rep from * once.

ROW 6: (knit with B; purl with A) [Tk1, Tp1] 3 times, C2kR, [Tk1, Tp1] 6 times, C2kL, [Tk1, Tp1] 3 times.

ROW 7: (knit with A; purl with B) *C2kR, [Tk1, Tp1] 4 times, C2kL; rep from * once.

ROW 8: (knit with B; purl with A) C2kL, C2kR, [Tk1, Tp1] 2 times, C2kR, C2kL, [Tk1, Tp1] 2 times, C2kL, C2kR.

ROW 9: (knit with A; purl with B) [Tk1, Tp1] 7 times, C2kL, [Tk1, Tp1] 7 times.

ROW 10: (knit with B; purl with A) Tk1, Tp1, C2kR, [Tk1, Tp1] 10 times, C2kL, Tk1, Tp1.

ROW 11: (knit with A; purl with B) *C2kL, [Tk1, Tp1] 4 times, C2kR; rep from * once.

ROW 12: (knit with B; purl with A) [C2kL] 2 times, [Tk1, Tp1] 2 times, C2kR, C2kL, [Tk1, Tp1] 2 times, [C2kR] 2 times.

ROW 13: (knit with A; purl with B) *Tk1, Tp1, C2kL, [Tk1, Tp1] 2 times, C2kR, Tk1, Tp1; rep from * once.

TRAVELING-STITCH DIAMOND LATTICE AND WIDE CABLE
SIDE 1: DIAMOND LATTICE (LIGHT, PATTERNING ON ODD ROWS)

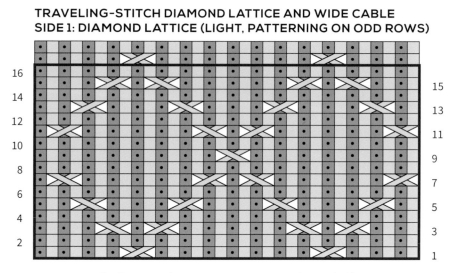

mult of 32 sts and 16 rows + 2; see page 120 for symbol key

TRAVELING-STITCH DIAMOND LATTICE AND WIDE CABLE
SIDE 2: WIDE CABLE (DARK, PATTERNING ON EVEN ROWS)

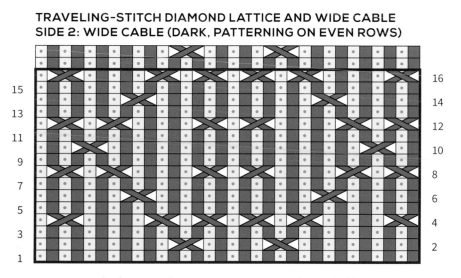

mult of 32 sts and 16 rows + 2; see page 120 for symbol key

ROW 14: (knit with B; purl with A) [Tk1, Tp1] 3 times, C2kL, [Tk1, Tp1] 6 times, C2kR, [Tk1, Tp1] 3 times.

ROW 15: (knit with A; purl with B) *[Tk1, Tp1] 2 times, C2kL, C2kR, [Tk1, Tp1] 2 times; rep from * once.

ROW 16: (knit with B; purl with A) C2kL, [Tk1, Tp1] 2 times, [C2kL, C2kR] 2 times, [Tk1, Tp1] 2 times, C2kR.

Repeat Rows 1–16 for pattern, then end by working Rows 1 and 2 once more to balance.

Crossover Cables, front ◀ | ▶ Crossover Cables, back

MIRRORED TRAVELING-STITCH CABLES

Traveling-stitch cable patterns can also be worked so that the pattern on the front is mirrored on the back. In these patterns, cables that cross to the left on the front cross to the right on the back, and vice versa.

CROSSOVER CABLES

SET-UP: Work Twigg st for 2 rows.

ROW 1: (knit with A; purl with B) [Tk1, Tp1] 2 times, CCR, [Tk1, Tp1] 8 times, CCR, [Tk1, Tp1] 2 times.

ROW 2 AND ALL EVEN-NUMBERED ROWS: (knit with B; purl with A) Work even in rib as established.

ROW 3: (knit with A; purl with B) Tk1, Tp1, CCR, [CCL] 2 times, [Tk1, Tp1] 2 times, [CCR] 2 times, CCL, Tk1, Tp1.

ROW 5: (knit with A; purl with B) CCR, [Tk1, Tp1] 2 times, [CCL] 2 times, [CCR] 2 times, [Tk1, Tp1] 2 times, CCL.

ROW 7: (knit with A; purl with B) [Tk1, Tp1] 7 times, CCR, [Tk1, Tp1] 7 times.

ROW 9: (knit with A; purl with B) CCL, [Tk1, Tp1] 2 times, [CCR] 2 times, [CCL] 2 times, [Tk1, Tp1] 2 times, CCR.

ROW 11: (knit with A; purl with B) Tk1, Tp1, CCL, [CCR] 2 times, [Tk1, Tp1] 2 times, [CCL] 2 times, CCR, Tk1, Tp1.

ROW 12: (knit with B; purl with A) Work even in rib as established.

Repeat Rows 1–12 for pattern, then work Rows 1 and 2 once more to balance.

CROSSOVER CABLES

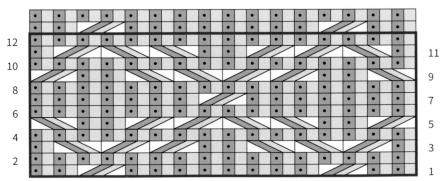

mult of 32 sts and 12 rows + 2; see page 120 for symbol key

2×2 Rib Variation Patterns

A variety of designs and textures stem from basic 2×2 rib patterns, including some of the thickest and some of the thinnest Twigg-stitch fabrics. For these patterns, I usually start with a single knit stitch to keep the yarns balanced and the edges neat.

The swatches in this section were worked with Cascade Yarns 220 Sport (100% wool; 164 yd [150 m]/50 g) in #8905 Robin Egg Blue (light blue; A) and #7818 Blue Velvet (dark blue; B).

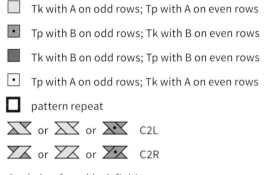

SYMBOL KEY FOR 2×2 RIB PATTERN CHARTS

Tk with A on odd rows; Tp with A on even rows

Tp with B on odd rows; Tk with B on even rows

Tk with B on odd rows; Tp with B on even rows

Tp with A on odd rows; Tk with A on even rows

pattern repeat

or ▨ or ▧ C2L

or ▨ or ▧ C2R

See below for cable definitions.

2×2 RIB ABBREVIATIONS

cn: cable needle

C2L: (cross 2 sts to the left) Working the 2 cable sts as established (Tk1 the knits, and Tp1 the purls) in the colors shown, slip 1 st onto a cn and hold in front, work 1 st, then work the st from the cn.

C2R: (cross 2 sts to the right) Working the 2 cable sts as established (Tk1 the knits, and Tp1 the purls) in the colors shown, slip 1 st onto a cn and hold in back, work 1 st, then work the st from the cn.

See below for a no-cable needle technique.

CROSSING STITCHES WITHOUT A CABLE NEEDLE

It's quite easy to work two-stitch cables without a cable needle.

CROSS TWO STITCHES TO THE LEFT

Take the right needle tip behind the first stitch on the left needle, then insert it into the second stitch on the left needle. Slip both stitches off the left needle, allowing the first stitch to drop in front of the work. Insert the left needle into the dropped stitch to catch it, then return the stitch on the right needle

to the left needle, and work the stitches in their new order.

CROSS TWO STITCHES TO THE RIGHT

Take the right needle tip in front of the first stitch on the left needle, then insert it into the second stitch on the left needle. Slip both stitches off the left needle, allowing the first stitch to drop behind the work. Insert the left needle into the dropped stitch to catch it, then return the stitch on the right needle to the left needle, and work the stitches in their new order.

Basic 2×2 Rib, front ◄ | ► *Basic 2×2 Rib, back*

Basic 2×2 Rib

This technique produces a very thick fabric. To add stripes, simply start the row using the opposite colors for the knit and purl stitches. Light knit ribs on one side will appear as dark knit ribs on the other and vice versa.

You can also add new colors by cutting the working yarn and joining a new color on one or both sides.

The color sequence for casting on is ABBA.

ROW 1: (knit with A; purl with B) *Tk1, Tp2, Tk1; rep from *.

ROW 2: (knit with B; purl with A) *Tp1, Tk2, Tp1; rep from *.

Repeat Rows 1 and 2 for pattern.

BASIC 2×2 RIB WITH STRIPES

This pattern creates two-row stripes. For different-width stripes, work as many rows as desired before switching the colors.

The color sequence for casting on is ABBA.

ROW 1: (knit with A; purl with B) *Tk1, Tp2, Tk1; rep from *.

ROW 2: (knit with B; purl with A) *Tp1, Tk2, Tp1; rep from *.

ROW 3: (knit with B; purl with A) Rep Row 1.

ROW 4: (knit with A; purl with B) Rep Row 2.

BASIC 2×2 RIB

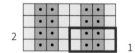

mult of 4 sts and 2 rows
see page 129 for symbol key

BASIC 2×2 RIB WITH STRIPES

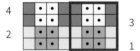

mult of 4 sts and 4 rows
see page 129 for symbol key

Herringbone, front ◄ │ ► *Herringbone, back*

Herringbone

Here, a two-color diagonal pattern is produced by staggering the 2x2 rib sequence one stitch every row. The surprisingly lightweight fabric is predominantly light on one side and predominantly dark on the other.

The color sequence for casting on is ABBA.

ROW 1: (knit with A; purl with B) *Tk1, Tp2, Tk1; rep from*.

ROW 2: (knit with B; purl with A) *Tp2, Tk2; rep from *.

ROW 3: (knit with A; purl with B) *Tp1, Tk2, Tp1; rep from *.

ROW 4: (knit with B; purl with A) *Tk2, Tp2; rep from *.

Repeat Rows 1–4 for pattern.

HERRINGBONE

4

2

3

1

mult of 4 sts and 4 rows
see page 129 for symbol key

Staggered Rib, front ◄ | ► *Staggered Rib, back*

Staggered Rib

In this variation, the pattern shifts one stitch every two rows, resulting in a thicker, springier fabric that is predominantly light on one side and predominantly dark on the other.

The color sequence for casting on is ABBA.

ROW 1: (knit with A; purl with B) *Tk1, Tp2, Tk1; rep from *.

ROW 2: (knit with B; purl with A) *Tp1, Tk2, Tp1; rep from *.

ROW 3: (knit with A; purl with B) *Tp2, Tk2; rep from *.

ROW 4: (knit with B; purl with A) *Tp2, Tk2; rep from *.

ROW 5: (knit with A; purl with B) *Tp1, Tk2, Tp1; rep from *.

ROW 6: (knit with B; purl with A) *Tk1, Tp2, Tk1; rep from *.

ROW 7: (knit with A; purl with B) *Tk2, Tp2; rep from *.

ROW 8: (knit with B; purl with A) *Tk2, Tp2; rep from *.

Repeat Rows 1–8 for pattern.

STAGGERED RIB

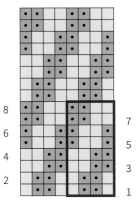

mult of 4 sts and 8 rows
see page 129 for symbol key

Basketweave, Colors Matched, front ◄ | ► *Basketweave, Colors Matched, back*

Basketweave

In basketweave patterns, the knit and purl stitches switch every two rows to produce a checkerboard effect in a fabric that's quite lightweight. Depending on how you hold the yarns, you can make a fabric that looks the same on both sides or a fabric that is predominantly light on one side and predominantly dark on the other.

COLORS MATCHED

In this version, each two-stitch column is always worked using the same color, but the knits and purls are switched every 2 rows. The fabric looks the same on both sides.

The color sequence for casting on is ABBA.

ROW 1: (knit with A; purl with B) *Tk1, Tp2, Tk1; rep from *.

ROW 2: (knit with B; purl with A) *Tp1, Tk2, Tp1; rep from *.

ROW 3: (knit with B; purl with A) *Tp1, Tk2, Tp1; rep from *.

ROW 4: (knit with A; purl with B) *Tk1, Tp2, Tk1; rep from *.

Repeat Rows 1–4 for pattern.

BASKETWEAVE WITH COLORS MATCHED

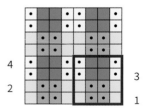

mult of 4 sts and 4 rows
see page 129 for symbol key

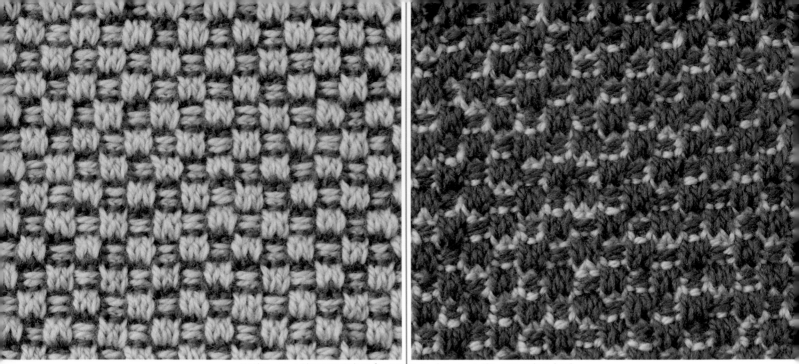

Basketweave Alternate Colors, front ◄ │ ► *Basketweave Alternate Colors, back*

ALTERNATE COLORS

In this version, the colors as well as the knits and purls are switched every two rows. The pattern is the same on both sides, but predominantly light on one side and predominantly dark on the other.

The color sequence for casting on is ABBA.

ROW 1: (knit with A; purl with B) *Tk1, Tp2, Tk1; rep from *.

ROW 2: (knit with B; purl with A) *Tp1, Tk2, Tp1; rep from *.

ROW 3: (knit with A; purl with B) *Tp1, Tk2, Tp1; rep from *.

ROW 4: (knit with B; purl with A) *Tk1, Tp2, Tk1; rep from *.

Repeat Rows 1–4 for pattern.

BASKETWEAVE WITH ALTERNATE COLORS

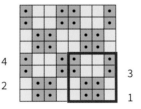

mult of 4 sts and 4 rows
see page 129 for symbol key

Honeycomb, front ◄ ❘ ► *Honeycomb, back*

Honeycomb

Honeycomb patterns result from working two-stitch cables every other row to shift the position of the knit (and purl) stitches. See page 129 for cable abbreviations.

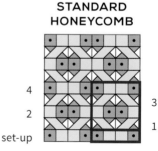

STANDARD HONEYCOMB

4
2
set-up

3
1

mult of 4 sts and 4 rows
see page 129 for symbol key

STANDARD HONEYCOMB

The colors used to knit and purl remain the same throughout to produce a wonderfully thick and warm fabric that's predominantly light on one side and predominantly dark on the other.

The color sequence for casting on is BAAB.

SET-UP ROW: (knit with B; purl with A) *Tk1, Tp2, Tk1; rep from *.

ROW 1: (knit with A; purl with B) *C2R, C2L; rep to end.

ROW 2: (knit with B; purl with A) *Tp1, Tk2, Tp1; rep from *.

ROW 3: (knit with A; purl with B) *C2L, C2R; rep from *.

ROW 4: (knit with B; purl with A) *Tk1, Tp2, Tk1; rep from *.

Repeat Rows 1–4 for pattern.

Honeycomb with a Twist, front ◀ | ▶ *Honeycomb with a Twist, back*

HONEYCOMB WITH A TWIST

In this version, the colors used to knit and purl remain the same throughout, but the cables are worked every row to produce a lattice look. This stitch pattern is the same on both sides of the dense fabric, but one side is predominantly light and the other is predominantly dark.

The color sequence for casting on is BAAB.

SET-UP ROW: (knit with B; purl with A) *Tk1, Tp2, Tk1; rep from *.

ROW 1: (knit with A; purl with B) Tp1, *C2R; rep from * to last st, Tp1.

ROW 2: (knit with B; purl with A) *C2L, C2R; rep from *.

ROW 3: (knit with A; purl with B) Tk1, *C2L; rep from * to last st, Tk1.

ROW 4: (knit with B; purl with A) *C2R, C2L; rep from *.

Repeat Rows 1–4 for pattern.

HONEYCOMB WITH A TWIST

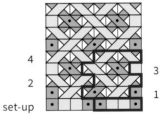

mult of 4 sts and 4 rows
see page 129 for symbol key

Lace Patterns

You can get beautiful lace effects by combining basic Twigg stitch with a variety of increases and decreases. Unlike many forms of "regular" lace, these patterns are equally lovely on both sides, although you will need to knit with thinner yarns to keep them lightweight.

The swatches in this section were worked with Cascade Yarns 220 Sport (100% wool; 164 yd [150 m]/50 g) in #8908 Anis (aqua; A) and #9420 Como Blue (teal; B).

SYMBOL KEY FOR LACE PATTERN CHARTS

☐	Tk with A on odd rows; Tp with A on even rows	➕	single-rib inc
▪	Tp with B on odd rows; Tk with B on even rows	○	ryo
■	Tk with B on odd rows; Tp with B on even rows	◻	work [Tp1, Tk1, Tp1] in same st
▪	Tp with A on odd rows; Tk with A on even rows	◻	switch 2 sts then kinc
╱	Tk2tog with A on odd rows; Tp2tog with A on even rows	◻	kinc
╱	Tp2tog with B on odd rows; Tk2tog with B on even rows	◻	switch 2 sts, knit-yo, Tp1, Tssk
╲	Tssk with A on odd rows; Tssptbl with A on even rows	◻	sl 1, switch 2 sts, return sl st to left needle, Tk2tog, Tp1, knit-yo
╲	Tssptbl with B on odd rows; Tssk with B on even rows		
⚹	Tk3tog with A on odd rows; Tp3tog with A on even rows	◪	C2kL
⚹	Tp3tog with B on odd rows; Tk3tog with B on even rows	○•○╱○	Double dec with yo's
⊙	knit-yo with A on odd rows; purl-yo with A on even rows		*See page 138 for abbreviations.*
▨	no stitch		
▢	pattern repeat		

LACE ABBREVIATIONS

cn: cable needle

C2kL: (cross 2 knit sts to the left) Slip 1 knit st onto a cn and hold in front of the work, slip the next st (a purl st) onto a cn and hold in back of the work, Tk1, then Tp1 from cn at back, then Tk1 from cn at front, then Tp1.

double dec with yo's: Arrange next 5 sts so the 2 purl sts are on a cn held in back of work, and the 3 knit sts are on the left needle. Sl 2 knit sts to right needle, pass first st over the second, return 1 knit st to left needle, pass second st on left needle over returned st—1 (center) knit st rem on left needle. Place first purl st from cn back onto left needle tip, knit-yo, Tp2tog, knit-yo, Tp1 from cn, knit-yo—5 sts made from 5 sts.

kinc: (knit increase) Work the next 2 sts as Tk1, Tp1, then Tk1 into the left leg of the knit st again (as for a branched inc; see page 39)—1 knit st inc'd.

knit-yo: Beginning with both yarns in back, bring just the knit yarn around the right needle knitwise to form a new st (not reverse-mounted).

purl-yo: Beginning with both yarns in front, bring just the purl yarn around the right needle purlwise to form a new st (not reverse-mounted).

Ldec: Tk1, then Tp3tog—4 sts dec'd to 2 sts; 2 sts of each color dec'd to 1 st of each color.

Rdec: Tk3tog, then Tp1—4 sts dec'd to 2 sts; 2 sts of each color dec'd to 1 st of each color.

ryo: (reverse yarnover) Bring both yarns from back to front over the top of the right needle tip and between the two needles to the back again to create a double-strand loop with a reverse mount. On the following row, work Tk1, Tp1 into the back of the double-strand loop—2 sts made from 2-strand ryo (see page 37).

single-rib inc: Insert the left needle tip from front to back under the pair of horizontal strands between the needles so that the knit yarn is to the right of the purl yarn. Twigg-knit the knit-color strand, then Twigg-purl the purl color strand—2 sts (one rib pair) inc'd, 1 st of each color (see page 38).

switch 2 sts: Exchange position of the next 2 stitches on the left needle without working them, crossing the knit st in front of the purl st.

Tk2tog: Twigg-knit 2 stitches together (1 of each color) using the knit yarn.

Tp2tog: Twigg-purl 2 stitches together (1 of each color) using the purl yarn.

Tk3tog: Twigg-knit 3 stitches together 2 knit stitches plus the purl stitch between them) using the knit yarn.

Tp3tog: Twigg-purl 3 stitches together (2 purl stitches plus the knit stitch between them) using the purl yarn.

Tssk: Slip 2 sts individually knitwise, hold needles tip to tip, then slip these 2 sts back onto the left needle and Twigg-knit them together through their back loops—1 st dec'd.

Tssptbl: Slip 2 sts individually knitwise, hold needles tip to tip, then slip these 2 sts back onto the left needle and Twigg-purl them together through the back loops—1 st dec'd.

Chevrons, front ◀ | ▶ *Chevrons, back*

Chevrons

For this scalloped effect, single-rib increases are worked in conjunction with Twigg-knit and Twigg-purl decreases in a two-row pattern. A striking effect is produced with the addition of stripes, which are easily added by working one or two rows with the yarns reversed (knit with B and purl with A on odd-numbered rows; knit with A and purl with B on even-numbered rows).

SET-UP ROW 1: (knit with A; purl with B) *Tk1, tp1; rep from *.

SET-UP ROW 2: (knit with B; purl with A) *Tk1, tp1; rep from *.

ROW 1: (knit with A; purl with B) Tk1, Tp1, *single-rib inc (see Lace Abbreviations), [Tk1, Tp1] 3 times, Tk3tog, Tp3tog, [Tk1 Tp1] 3 times, single-rib inc, Tk1, Tp1; rep from *.

ROW 2: (knit with B; purl with A) *Tk1, Tp1; rep from*.

Repeat Rows 1 and 2 for pattern; do not repeat the set-up rows.

CHEVRONS

mult of 20 sts + 2 and 2 rows
see page 137 for symbol key

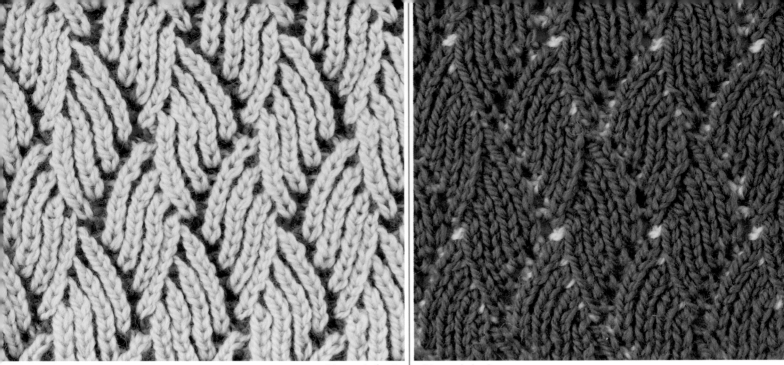

Diamonds, front ◄ | ► *Diamonds, back*

Diamonds

This interlocking diamond pattern results from reverse yarnovers and directional decreases on odd-numbered rows. Alternate rows are simply worked in the established rib pattern. Although the pattern is similar on both sides of the fabric, one side is predominantly light while the other is predominantly dark. Motifs that slant to the right on one side slant to the left on the other side and vice versa.

ROW 1: (knit with A; purl with B) [Tk1, Tp1] 3 times, *ryo, Ldec, [Tk1, Tp1] 3 times; rep from * to last 4 sts, ryo, Ldec.

ROW 2 AND ALL EVEN-NUMBERED ROWS: (knit with B; purl with A) Work even in rib as established, working Tk1, Tp1 into each ryo.

ROW 3: (knit with A; purl with B) Rdec, Tk1, Tp1, *ryo, Tk1, Tp1, Ldec, [Tk1, Tp1] 2 times; rep from * to last 4 sts, ryo, [Tk1, Tp1] 2 times.

ROW 5: (knit with A; purl with B) [Tk1, Tp1] 2 times, *ryo, [Tk1, Tp1] 2 times, Ldec, Tk1, Tp1; rep from * to last 6 sts, ryo, Tk1, Tp1, Ldec.

ROW 7: (knit with A; purl with B) Rdec, *ryo, [Tk1 Tp1] 3 times, Ldec; rep from * to last 6 sts, ryo, [Tk1, Tp1] 3 times.

DIAMONDS

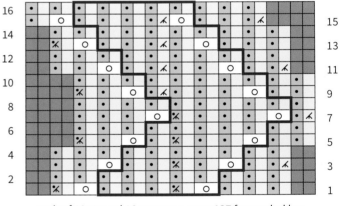

mult of 10 sts and 16 rows; see page 137 for symbol key

ROW 9: (knit with A; purl with B) [Tk1, Tp1] 2 times, *ryo, [Tk1, Tp1] 3 times, Rdec; rep from * to last 6 sts, ryo, Tk1, Tp1, Ldec.

ROW 11: (knit with A; purl with B) Rdec, Tk1, Tp1, *ryo, [Tk1, Tp1] 2 times, Rdec, Tk1, Tp1; rep from * to last 4 sts, ryo, [Tk1, Tp1] 2 times.

ROW 13: (knit with A; purl with B) [Tk1, Tp1] 3 times, *ryo, Tk1, Tp1, Rdec, [Tk1, Tp1] 2 times; rep from * to last 4 sts, ryo, Ldec.

Leaves, front ◄ | ► Leaves, back

ROW 15: (knit with A; purl with B) Rdec, [Tk1, Tp1] 2 times, *ryo, Rdec, [Tk1, Tp1] 3 times; rep from * to last 2 sts, ryo, Tk1, Tp1.

ROW 16: (knit with B; purl with A) Work even in rib as established.

Repeat Rows 1–16 for pattern.

Leaves

This pattern is a smaller version of the one used for the Mothwing Scarf on page 90. The tessellated motifs result from reverse yarnovers and directional single and double decreases on odd-numbered rows. Alternate rows are simply worked in the rib pattern as established. The pattern is similar on both sides of the fabric, but one side is predominantly light while the other is predominantly dark.

ROW 1: (knit with A; purl with B) [Tk1, Tp1] 2 times, *Tk1, Tp2tog, ryo, Tk2tog, Tp1, Tk1, Tp1; rep from * to last 2 sts, Tk1, Tp1.

ROWS 2, 4, AND 6: (knit with B; purl with A) Work even in rib as established, working Tk1, Tp1 into each ryo.

ROW 3: (knit with A; purl with B) Tk1, Tp1, Tk1, Tp3tog, ryo, *Tk1, Tp1, ryo, Tk3tog, Tp3tog, ryo; rep from * to last 8 sts, Tk1, Tp1, ryo, Tk3tog, Tp1, Tk1, Tp1.

LEAVES

mult of 8 sts + 6 and 8 rows; see page 137 for symbol key

ROW 5: (knit with A; purl with B) [Tk1, Tp1] 4 times, *Tk1, Tp2tog, ryo, Tk2tog, Tp1, Tk1, Tp1; rep from * to last 6 sts, [Tk1, Tp1] 3 times.

ROW 7: (knit with A; purl with B) [Tk1, Tp1] 2 times, *ryo, Tk3tog, Tp3tog, ryo, Tk1, Tp1; rep from * last 2 sts, Tk1, Tp1.

ROW 8: (knit with B; purl with A) Work even in rib as established.

Repeat Rows 1–8 for pattern.

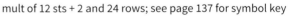
Shells, front ◀ ｜ ▶ Shells, back

Shells

This rounded shell pattern results from reverse yarnovers and mostly left-leaning decreases on odd-numbered rows. Alternate rows are simply worked in the established rib pattern. Although the pattern is similar on both sides of the fabric, one side is light while the other is dark, and motifs that curve to the right on one side curve to the left on the other and vice versa.

ROW 1: (knit with A; purl with B) Tk1, Tp1, *ryo, Rdec, [Tk1, Tp1] 4 times; rep from *.

ROW 2 AND ALL EVEN-NUMBERED ROWS: (knit with B; purl with A) Work even in rib as established, working Tk1, Tp1 into each ryo.

ROW 3: (knit with A; purl with B) Tk1, Tp1, *ryo, Ldec, [Tk1, Tp1] 4 times; rep from *.

ROW 5: (knit with A; purl with B) Tk1, Tp1, *ryo, Tk1, Tp1, Ldec, [Tk1, Tp1] 3 times; rep from *.

ROW 7: (knit with A; purl with B) Tk1, Tp1, *ryo, [Tk1, Tp1] 2 times, Ldec, [Tk1, Tp1] 2 times; rep from *.

ROW 9: (knit with A; purl with B) Tk1, Tp1, *ryo, [Tk1, Tp1] 3 times, Ldec, Tk1, Tp1; rep from *.

ROW 11: (knit with A; purl with B) Tk1, Tp1, *ryo, [Tk1, Tp1] 4 times, Ldec; rep from *.

SHELLS

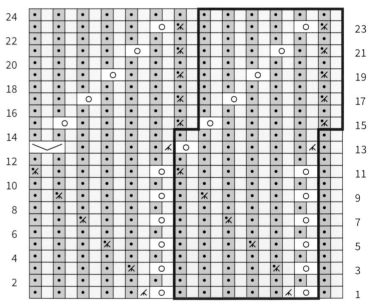

mult of 12 sts + 2 and 24 rows; see page 137 for symbol key

ALLOVER LACE RIGHT-SLOPING

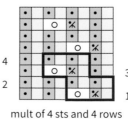

mult of 4 sts and 4 rows
see page 137 for symbol key

ALLOVER LACE LEFT-SLOPING

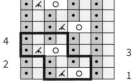

mult of 4 sts and 4 rows
see page 137 for symbol key

142　Twigg Stitch

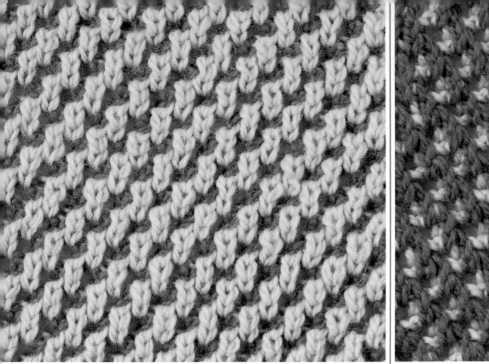

Allover Lace, Right-Sloping, front ◄ ▎▶ *Allover Lace, Right-Sloping, back*

ROW 13: (knit with A; purl with B) Tk1, Tp1, *Rdec, [Tk1, Tp1] 4 times, ryo; rep from * to last 12 sts, Rdec, [Tk1, Tp1] 3 times, Tk1, work [Tp1, Tk1, Tp1] in the last st.

ROW 15: (knit with A; purl with B) *Ldec, [Tk1, Tp1] 4 times, ryo; rep from * to last 2 sts, Tk1, Tp1.

ROW 17: (knit with A; purl with B) *Ldec, [Tk1, Tp1] 3 times, ryo, Tk1, Tp1; rep from * to last 2 sts, Tk1, Tp1.

ROW 19: (knit with A; purl with B) *Ldec, [Tk1, Tp1] 2 times, ryo, [Tk1, Tp1] 2 times; rep from * to last 2 sts, Tk1, Tp1.

ROW 21: (knit with A; purl with B) *Ldec, Tk1, Tp1, ryo, [Tk1, Tp1] 3 times; rep from * to last 2 sts, Tk1, Tp1.

ROW 23: (knit with A; purl with B) *Ldec, ryo, [Tk1, Tp1] 4 times; rep from * to last 2 sts, Tk1, Tp1.

ROW 24: (knit with B; purl with A) Work even in rib as established.

Repeat Rows 1–24 for pattern.

Allover Lace

This small allover pattern results from reverse yarnovers coupled with purl-three-together (p3tog) decreases. The direction of slant depends on how the decreases are worked—purlwise for a right slant; knitwise for a left slant.

RIGHT-SLOPING PATTERN

In this version, decreases are worked purlwise for a pattern that slants to the right when viewed from the light side. The two sides are similar, but the pattern slants in the opposite direction on the dark side.

ROW 1: (knit with A; purl with B) *Ldec, ryo; rep from * to last 4 sts, [Tk1, Tp1] 2 times.

ROW 2: (knit with B; purl with A) Work even in rib as established.

ROW 3: (knit with A; purl with B) Tk1, Tp1, *Ldec, ryo; rep from * to last 2 sts, Tk1, Tp1.

ROW 4: (knit with B; purl with A) Work even in rib as established.

Repeat Rows 1–4 for pattern.

LEFT-SLOPING PATTERN

In this version, decreases are worked knitwise for a pattern that slants to the left when viewed from the light side. The two sides are similar, but the pattern slants in the opposite direction on the dark side.

ROW 1: (knit with A; purl with B) Tk1, Tp1, *ryo, Rdec; rep from * to last 2 sts, Tk1, Tp1.

ROW 2: (knit with B; purl with A) Work even in rib as established.

ROW 3: (knit with A; purl with B) [Tk1, Tp1] 2 times, *ryo, Rdec; rep from *.

ROW 4: Work even in rib as established.

Repeat Rows 1–4 for pattern.

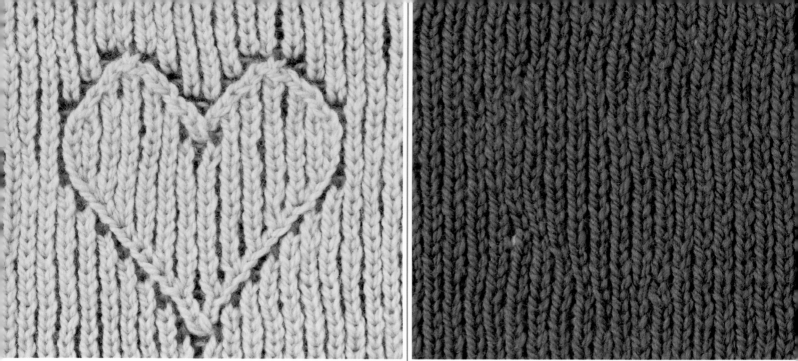

Heart, front ◄ | ► *Heart, back*

Heart

You can combine directional increases and decreases with simple cables to make a host of designs, such as the heart motif shown here. The pattern appears just on the light side against a dark foundation. The dark side appears as basic Twigg stitch.

ROW 1: (knit with A; purl with B) Work in basic Twigg st.

ROW 2: (knit with B; purl with A) [Tk1, Tp1] 7 times, Tssk, purl-yo, Tk1, purl-yo, Tk2tog, Tp1, [Tk1, Tp1] 6 times.

ROW 3: (knit with A; purl with B) [Tk1, Tp1] 7 times, C2kL, [Tk1, Tp1] 7 times.

ROW 4 AND ALL EVEN-NUMBERED ROWS THROUGH ROW 16: (knit with B; purl with A) Work even in rib as established.

ROW 5: (knit with A; purl with B) [Tk1, Tp1] 5 times, Tk1, Tp2tog, switch 2 sts then kinc, Tp1, kinc, Tssptbl, [Tk1, Tp1] 6 times.

ROW 7: (knit with A; purl with B) [Tk1, Tp1] 4 times, Tk1, Tp2tog, switch 2 sts then kinc, Tp1, [Tk1, Tp1] 2 times, kinc, Tssptbl, [Tk1, Tp1] 5 times.

ROW 9: (knit with A; purl with B) [Tk1, Tp1] 3 times, Tk1, Tp2tog, switch 2 sts then kinc, Tp1, [Tk1, Tp1] 4 times, kinc, Tssptbl, [Tk1, Tp1] 4 times.

ROW 11: (knit with A; purl with B) [Tk1, Tp1] 2 times, Tk1, Tp2tog, switch 2 sts then kinc, Tp1, [Tk1, Tp1] 6 times, kinc, Tssptbl, [Tk1, Tp1] 3 times.

ROW 13: (knit with A; purl with B) Tk1, Tp1, Tk1, Tp2tog, switch 2 sts then kinc, Tp1, [Tk1, Tp1] 8 times, kinc, Tssptbl, [Tk1, Tp1] 2 times.

ROW 15: (knit with A; purl with B) Tk1, Tp2tog, switch 2 sts, kinc, Tp1, [Tk1, Tp1] 10 times, kinc, Tssptbl, Tk1, Tp1.

HEART

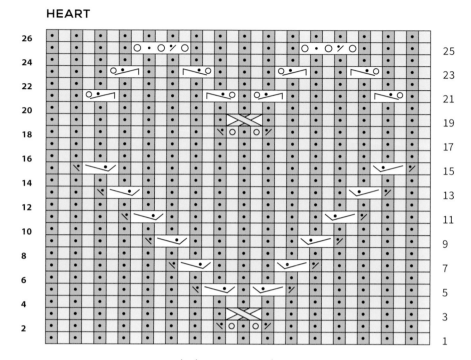

worked over 32 sts and 26 rows
see page 137 for symbol key

ROW 17: (knit with A; purl with B) Work even in rib as established.

ROWS 18 AND 19: Rep Rows 2 and 3.

ROWS 20, 22, AND 24: (knit with B; purl with A) Work even in rib as established.

ROW 21: (knit with A; purl with B) Tk1, Tp1, *switch 2 sts, knit-yo, Tp1, Tssk, Tp1, [Tk1, Tp1] 3 times, sl 1, switch 2 sts, return slipped st to left needle, Tk2tog, Tp1, knit-yo, Tp1; rep from * once, Tk1, Tp1.

ROW 23: (knit with A; purl with B) *[Tk1, Tp1] 2 times, switch 2 sts, knit-yo, Tp1, Tssk, Tp1, Tk1, Tp1, sl 1, switch 2 sts, return slipped st to left needle, Tk2tog, Tp1, knit-yo, Tp1; rep from * once, [Tk1, Tp1] 2 times.

ROW 25: (knit with A; purl with B) *[Tk1, Tp1] 3 times, work double dec with yo's over next 5 sts (see Lace Abbreviations), Tp1, Tk1, Tp1; rep from * once, [Tk1, Tp1] 2 times.

ROW 26: Work even in rib as established.

NOTES

At the beginning of each row, bring the knit yarn down in front of the purl yarn, under it, and into working position. Doing so creates the twisted loops in between the two edge stitches that will be used later for picking up stitches (see page 41). ● To identify the double loops for picking up stitches, view the selvedge edge—the two end stitches of each row appear as a pair of side-by-side knit stitches (one of each color). Gently separate these two columns of knit stitches so you can see the "ladder" of twisted double strands between them. When picking up stitches, slip the left needle under every other twisted double strand (where the knit color twists over the purl color) to place the double loop on the needle (see page 44). ● Place a removable stitch marker around the two yarns between units to indicate where to begin picking up stitches for units in the following tier.

Entrelac

Twigg stitch is very effective when used for entrelac, a technique that builds tiers of right- and left-slanting units on top of one another.

Twigg-stitch entrelac does not have the raised texture of the regular technique, but it creates a lovely woven effect while giving a truly two-sided result. Triangles are worked at the base, sides, and top to form straight edges.

The instructions that follow are based on blocks that are eighteen stitches wide and seventeen rows high, but the pattern can be customized for a different number of stitches and rows by following these guidelines:

ABBREVIATIONS FOR ENTRELAC PATTERNS

Tp&k: Tp1 as usual, then Tk1 into the back of same st—1 knit st inc'd.

Tk&p: Tk1 as usual, then Tp1 into the same st—1 knit st inc'd.

Join: (worked over the last 2 sts of the unit and first st of next unit) Sl 1 (the knit st), switch the positions of the next 2 sts, crossing the knit st in front, return the slipped st and switched sts to the left needle, Tssk, Tp1.

Pick up 18 sts: Working from the bottom of the slope up to the right needle tip, insert the left needle into the double loop held on the st holder and then under every other twisted double loop between the 2 edge sts (see Notes and page 44) until there are a total of 9 double loops on the left needle. To complete the first row, work1 row of double knitting (the yarn will not twist between the stitches on this row) by holding the knit and purl yarns the opposite of how you'd hold

them for basic Twigg-stitch (the knit yarn in front and the purl yarn at back if tensioning both yarns in the same hand). Work (k1 with knit yarn, p1 with purl yarn) in each double loop (1 rib made in each loop) for a total of 18 sts, then remove the marker from the last double loop.

Tk2tog: Twigg-knit 2 stitches together using the knit yarn.

Tssk: Slip 2 sts individually knitwise, hold needles tip to tip, then slip these 2 sts back onto the left needle and Twigg-knit them together through their back loops—1 st dec'd.

Tp2tog: Twigg-purl 2 stitches together using the purl yarn.

Tk3tog: Twigg-knit 3 stitches together using the knit yarn.

Tp3tog: Twigg-purl 3 stitches together using the purl yarn.

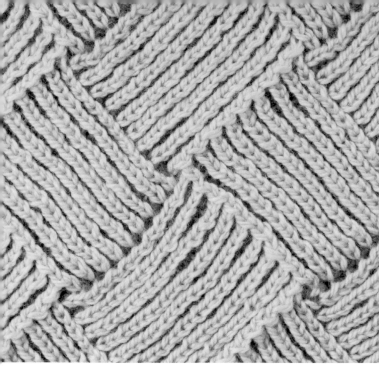 

Entrelac, front ◄ │ ► *Entrelac, back*

○ The row count in each square unit is always one less than its stitch count (for example, a square of ten stitches is worked over nine rows).

○ Work the base triangles until they contain one more stitch than you'll need for the square units (eleven-stitch triangles for ten-stitch squares) and use the extra stitch to begin the next triangle. The last triangle of the tier should contain two extra stitches (twelve stitches for a ten-stitch square).

○ When picking up stitches, pick up half as many double-yarn loops as the number of stitches for the new unit (five double loops for a ten-stitch square).

○ Make a copy of the instructions below and write in your new stitch and row numbers for each unit.

Base Triangles
(left-slanting on light side)

FIRST TRIANGLE

SET-UP: Holding both yarns tog, make a slipknot and place it on the left needle (this slipknot does not count as a st and will be removed later). Using the e-wrap method (see page 14), CO 1 st with B, then CO 1 st with A.

ROW 1: (knit with A; purl with B) Tk1, Tp&k—1 st inc'd. Drop the slipknot (on the first triangle only).

ROW 2: (knit with B; purl with A) Tk&p, work to end in established rib—1 st inc'd.

ROW 3: (knit with A; purl with B) Work in rib as established to last st, Tp&k—1 st inc'd.

ROWS 4–16: Rep Rows 2 and 3 six more times, then rep Row 2 once more—18 sts.

ROW 17: (knit with A; purl with B) Work in rib as established to last st, Tp&k—19 sts.

SECOND AND ALL FOLLOWING TRIANGLES

SET-UP ROW: (knit with B; purl with A) With dark side facing, Tk&p, turn work, leaving the rem 18 sts of the previous triangle unworked.

ROWS 1–17: Work as for first triangle, working even-numbered rows only to the end of this triangle; do not work across the sts of any previously completed triangles.

Repeat the second triangle instructions for as many triangles as desired, working the last st in Row 17 of the final triangle as foll: Tp1 as usual, then work [Tk1 into the back and Tp1 as usual] both into the same st—20 sts in last triangle and 18 sts in all other triangles.

> **note:** Diagram 1 on page 148 shows the arrangement with three base triangles; the swatch in the photograph has only two base triangles.

Tier 1 (right-slanting on light side)

This tier and all following odd-numbered tiers are worked with a left-side triangle, square units in the middle, and a right-side triangle (see Diagram 2).

LEFT-SIDE TRIANGLE

ROW 1: (knit with B; purl with A) With B side facing, work join over 3 sts as described on page 146, sl 1 with both yarns in front, turn work.

ROW 2: (knit with A; purl with B) Tk2tog, work as established to last st of triangle, Tp&k.

ROW 3: (knit with B; purl with A) Tk&p, work to last 2 sts of this unit, join, sl 1 with both yarns in front, turn work.

ROWS 4–16: Rep Rows 2 and 3 six times, then rep Row 2 once more—17 sts in side triangle, 2 sts rem to be joined in next unit.

ROW 17: (knit with B; purl with A) Tk&p, work to last 2 sts of this unit, work join ending Tp2tog instead of Tp1—18 sts in completed unit; no sts rem from unit being joined. Do not turn.

SQUARE

Pm around the two working yarns.

ROW 1: (A in knit position; B in purl position) With B side still facing, pick up 9 loops and work 18 sts in double knitting as described on page 146, sl next 2 sts purlwise with yarn in front, turn work.

ROW 2: (knit with A; purl with B) Tk3tog, work 17 sts as established, turn work.

ROW 3: (knit with B; purl with A) Work 16 sts as established, work join over next 3 sts, sl 1 with both yarns in front, turn work.

ROW 4: (knit with A; purl with B) Tk2tog, work rem 17 sts as established, turn work.

ROWS 5–16: Rep Rows 3 and 4 six more times—18 sts in this square, 2 sts rem to be joined in next unit.

ROW 17: (knit with B; purl with A) Work 16 sts as established, work join ending Tp2tog instead of Tp1—18 sts in completed square; no sts rem from unit being joined.

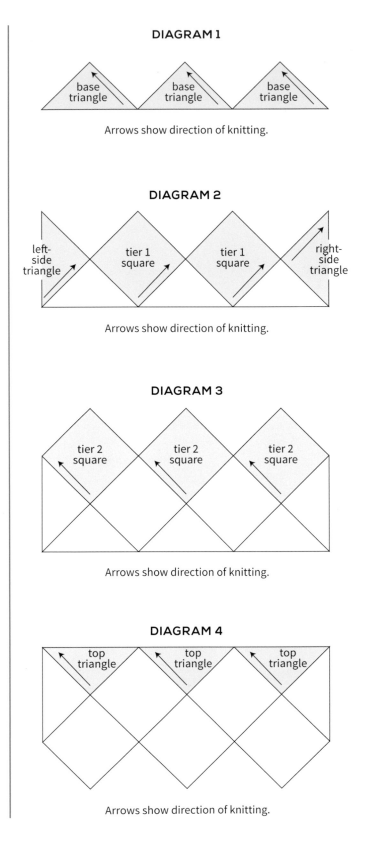

DIAGRAM 1

base triangle | base triangle | base triangle

Arrows show direction of knitting.

DIAGRAM 2

left-side triangle | tier 1 square | tier 1 square | right-side triangle

Arrows show direction of knitting.

DIAGRAM 3

tier 2 square | tier 2 square | tier 2 square

Arrows show direction of knitting.

DIAGRAM 4

top triangle | top triangle | top triangle

Arrows show direction of knitting.

-To continue with more squares, do not turn, pm around the two working yarns, then work Rows 1–17 again for the next 18-st square, joining the square to the live sts of the next unit as it is worked. After completing the last square, do not turn the work.

RIGHT-SIDE TRIANGLE

> **note:** For the very first right-side triangle, pick up two sts from the CO corner instead of from a marked loop.

Pm around the two working yarns.

ROW 1: (A in knit position; B in purl position) With B side still facing, pick up 18 sts along the side of the last unit as before, turn work.

ROW 2: (knit with A; purl with B) Work as established to end of triangle; do not work across the sts of any previously completed units.

ROW 3: (knit with B; purl with A) Work as established to last 3 sts, Tp3tog—2 sts dec'd.

ROWS 4–17: Rep Rows 2 and 3 seven more times—2 sts rem.

ROW 18: (knit with A; purl with B) Tk1, Tp1. Do not turn work.

Tier 2 (left-slanting on light side)

This tier and all following even-numbered tiers are worked with only square units (see Diagram 3).

SQUARE

Pm around the two working yarns.

ROW 1: (B in knit position; A in purl position) With A side facing, pick up 18 sts along the side of the unit from the previous tier, sl 2 sts of next unit purlwise with both yarns in front, turn work—20 sts on needle, including 2 triangle sts.

ROW 2: (knit with B; purl with A) Tk3tog, work 16 sts established, Tp3tog—18 sts in this square.

ROWS 3–17: Using the yarns the other way around (knit with A and purl with B on odd rows; knit with B and purl with A on even rows), work as for Rows 3–17 of square in Tier 2.

To continue with more squares, do not turn, pm around the two working yarns, then work Rows 1–17 again for as many squares as desired, working the last st of the join in Row 17 of the final square by inserting the right needle into the last 2 sts as if to Tp2tog and working Tp1, Tk1, Tp1 into them—20 sts in last unit: 18 square sts and 2 sts to use for left side triangle at start of next tier.

Tier 3 (right-slanting on light side)

Turn work so dark side is facing. Work as for Tier 1, with a left-side triangle, the desired number of squares, and then a right-side triangle.

Additional Tiers

Continue in this manner, alternating tiers of left- and right-slanting units, for the desired length, ending with an odd-numbered tier.

Top Triangles
(left-slanting on light side)

This tier produces triangles that fill the gaps at the top (see Diagram 4).

ROW 1: (B in knit position; A in purl position) Pick up 16 sts by placing 8 double loops from the side of the unit below (omitting the double loop at top of slope near the working yarns) on the needle—18 sts on needle, including 2 triangle sts. Sl 2 sts of next unit purlwise with both yarns in front, turn work.

ROW 2: (knit with B; purl with A) Tk3tog, work as established to last 3 sts, Tp3tog—2 sts dec'd.

ROW 3: (knit with A; purl with B) Work as established to last 2 sts of block, join as before, sl 1 with both yarns in front, turn work.

ROW 4: (knit with B; purl with A) Tk2tog, work even as established to last 3 sts, Tp3tog—2 sts dec'd.

ROWS 5–16: Rep Rows 3 and 4 six more times—2 sts on the block.

ROW 17: (knit with A; purl with B) Join, ending Tp2tog instead of Tp1—2 triangle sts rem. Do not turn.

To continue with more top triangles, rep Rows 1–17 until only 2 sts of the final top triangle rem. Cut yarns, then pull both yarns through both sts to fasten off.

Patterns with Unbalanced Color Use

Most of the patterns in this dictionary use the light and dark yarns at the same rate and are based on regular ribs.

In the following patterns, the two yarns are often used in unequal amounts on each row, and some variations in the rib pattern are explored. For this reason, it's best if you work these patterns by holding one yarn in each hand (see page 11). Unless otherwise directed, use the yarn held in your left hand for the knit stitches and use the yarn held in your right hand for the purl stitches.

The swatches in this section were worked with Cascade Yarns 220 Sport (100% wool; 164 yd [150 m]/50 g) in #8903 Primavera (lime; A) and #8267 Forest Green (dark green; B).

SYMBOL KEY FOR UNBALANCED COLOR USE PATTERN CHARTS

▢	Tk with A on odd rows and all rnds; Tp with A on even rows
▪	Tp with B on odd rows and all rnds ; Tk with B on even rows
▨	Tk with B on odd rows and all rnds; Tp with B on even rows
▫	Tp with A on odd rows and all rnds; Tk with A on even rows
K	Knit with A on even rnds; purl with A on even rows, holding B down
P	purl with B on odd rows and all rnds, holding B down
K	purl with B on even rows
▤	knit with A holding B in front on odd rows; purl with A holding B in back on even rows
▪	purl with B holding A in back on odd rows; knit with B holding A in front on even rows
◢	knit with A placing left needle behind B on odd rows and all rnds
◣	knit with B placing left needle behind A on odd rows and all rnds
◥	knit with A placing left needle behind B on even rows
☐	pattern repeat

See Abbreviations for definitions.

UNBALANCED COLOR USE ABBREVIATIONS

Tk: Twigg-knit so that the knit yarn traps the purl yarn.

Tp: Twigg-purl so that the purl yarn traps the knit yarn.

knit: work 1 regular knit stitch using the knit yarn, leaving the purl yarn at the back of the work to prevent it being trapped, then return the purl yarn to its usual position.

purl: work 1 regular purl stitch using the purl yarn, holding the knit yarn down in front of the work to prevent it being trapped, then return the knit yarn to its usual position.

place left needle tip behind: Place the left needle tip behind the strand of the indicated yarn so that the yarn sits next to the first st on the left needle, then work the strand together with the next st using the other color.

Wide Rib, front ◀ | ▶ *Wide Rib, back*

Wide Rib

For this four-stitch pattern repeat, work three stitches in regular Twigg st and the fourth as a regular purl stitch worked without trapping the knit yarn. The result is that a bit more of the purl yarn than the knit yarn is used on each row. It takes several rows for the pattern to emerge. The fabric looks the same on both sides, but one side is predominantly light and the other is predominantly dark.

WIDE RIB WORKED IN ROWS

ROW 1: (knit with A in the left hand; purl with B in the right hand) *Tp1, Tk1, Tp1, p1 with B while holding the knit yarn down in front of the work to prevent it from being trapped, return the purl yarn to its usual position; rep from * to last st, Tp1.

ROW 2: (knit with B; purl with A) Work as for Row 1, but switch the yarns to knit with B and purl with A.

Repeat Rows 1 and 2 for pattern.

WIDE RIB WORKED IN ROUNDS

To begin, cast on a multiple of 4 sts and join for working in rnds. Always bring A in front of B when switching yarns between rnds.

RND 1: (knit with A in left hand; purl with B in right hand) *Tp1, Tk1, Tp1, p1 with B while holding the knit yarn down in front of the work to prevent it from being trapped, then return the yarns to their Twigg-stitch positions; rep from *.

RND 2: (knit with A in right hand; purl with B in left hand) *Place left needle tip behind yarn B (see Stitch Guide) and knit yarn B together with the next st using A, k1 with A without trapping B at the back, place left needle tip behind yarn B and knit yarn B together with the next st using A, bring both yarns forward, then p1 with B in the left hand (without trapping A); rep from *.

Repeat Rnds 1 and 2 for pattern.

**WIDE RIB
WORKED IN ROWS**

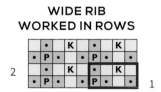

mult of 4 sts + 1 and 2 rows

**WIDE RIB
WORKED IN ROUNDS**

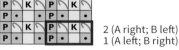

2 (A right; B left)
1 (A left; B right)

mult of 4 sts and 2 rnds

Ladder Rib, front ◄ | ► Ladder Rib, back

Ladder Rib

A mistake stitch (see page 112) worked in the center of a three-stitch rib creates a ladder effect that's the same on both sides of the fabric, but one side is predominantly light and the other is predominantly dark. A mistake stitch is worked by holding the purl yarn in the front when working a knit stitch, or by holding the knit yarn in back while working a purl stitch.

ROW 1: (knit with A; purl with B) *Tk1, bring just the purl yarn to the front, mistake k1, return the purl yarn to the back, Tk1, Tp1, bring just the knit yarn to the back, mistake p1, return the knit yarn to the front, Tp1; rep from*.

ROW 2: (knit with B; purl with A) Work as for Row 1, but switch the yarns to knit with B and purl with A.

Repeat Rows 1 and 2 for pattern.

LADDER RIB

2

1

mult of 6 sts and 2 rows
see page 150 for symbol key

Checkered Ladder, front ◄ | ► *Checkered Ladder, back*

Checkered Ladder

In this eight-row variation, the ribs shift every four rows to produce a checkerboard effect. The two sides of the fabric look the same, but the knit stitches are light on one side and dark on the other.

ROWS 1 AND 3: (knit with A; purl with B) *Tk1, bring just the purl yarn to the front, mistake k1, return the purl yarn to the back, Tk1, Tp1, bring just the knit yarn to the back, mistake p1, return the knit yarn to the front, Tp1; rep from*.

ROWS 2 AND 4: (knit with B; purl with A) Work as for Row 1, but switch the yarns to knit with B and purl with A.

ROWS 5 AND 7: (knit with A; purl with B) *Tp1, bring just the knit yarn to the back, mistake p1, return the knit yarn to the front, Tp1, Tk1, bring just the purl yarn to the front, mistake k1, return the purl yarn to the back, Tk1, rep from *.

ROWS 6 AND 8: (knit with B; purl with A) Work as for Row 5, but switch the yarns to knit with B and purl with A.

Repeat Rows 1–8 for pattern.

CHECKERED LADDER

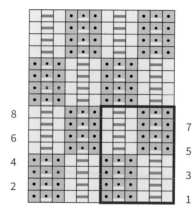

mult of 6 sts and 8 rows
see page 150 for symbol key

Color Play, front ◀ | ▶ *Color Play, back*

Color Play

This unique pattern produces vertical stripes on one side of the fabric and horizontal stripes on the other. It's based on regular Twigg stitch, but you work three stitches with the color held the right hand, then one stitch with the color held in the left hand on every row. Because this pattern involves knitting and purling with both hands, it may feel complicated at first, but it will become easier as the pattern grows and you can read your knitting. Vertical stripes form on the odd-numbered row side, horizontal stripes on the even-numbered row side.

COLOR PLAY WORKED IN ROWS

> note: Always take the yarn to be held in the left hand under the other yarn at the beginning of each row (page 41).

ROW 1: (A in left hand; B in right hand), *Tk1 with A, Tp1 with B, place left needle tip behind yarn A (see Stitch Guide) and knit A together with the next st using B, Tp1 with B; rep from *.

ROW 2: (A in right hand; B in left hand) *Place left needle tip behind yarn B and knit B together with the next st using A, bring both yarns to the front, p1 with B (without trapping A), bring both yarns to the back, place left needle tip behind yarn B and knit it together with the next st using A, Tp1 with A; rep from *.

Repeat Rows 1 and 2 for pattern.

COLOR PLAY WORKED IN ROUNDS

This forms vertical stripes on the outside of the tube and horizontal stripes on the inside.

> note: Always bring B across in front of A when switching yarns between rounds.

RND 1: (A in left hand; B in right hand) *Tk1 with A, Tp1 with B, place left needle tip behind yarn A (see Stitch Guide) and knit A together with the next st using B, Tp1 with B; rep from *.

RND 2: (B in left hand; A in right hand) *Place left needle tip behind yarn B and knit B together with next st using A, Tp1 with A, Tk1 with B, Tp1 with A; rep from *.

Repeat Rnds 1 and 2 for pattern.

COLOR PLAY WORKED IN ROWS

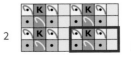

mult of 4 sts and 2 rows
see page 150 for symbol key

COLOR PLAY WORKED IN ROUNDS

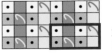

2 (A right; B left)
1 (A left; B right)

mult of 4 sts and 2 rnds
see page 150 for symbol key

Colorwork

Colorwork patterns, such as those created by color stranding or double knitting, can be worked in Twigg stitch as well. The patterns are produced by switching the knit and purl colors, usually according to a charted pattern.

To work the color-switch stitches, you'll need to change the positions of the light (A) and dark (B) yarns in your hands at every color change. Although this may seem tedious, especially when there are a lot of changes, it results in the most consistent tension and even stitches. If you prefer, you can hold the yarns the same way throughout and just switch between knitting and purling with each as necessary to maintain the pattern and being careful to get the correct twist between the stitches. However, take care that this approach doesn't alter your tension.

The most important thing to remember when working color patterns is that you'll need to be mindful of how the yarns twist around each other at the color changes, especially for patterns worked in the round. When you change colors, you can add an extra twist between them, or you can omit the twist. For a balanced fabric and to prevent the yarns getting irretrievably tangled, you'll need to do both.

You can either add an extra twist at the beginning of the pattern stitches, then omit the twist when returning to the original background color assignments, or you can omit the twist at the beginning of the pattern stitches, then add an extra twist when returning to the original colors. How you choose to work only matters when the color changes are stacked one above another on successive rows. One method will cause the stitches to sit a little farther apart; the other will cause them to sit just a little closer together. When stacked vertically over two or more consecutive rows, both can produce a noticeable "wiggle" in the rib. To prevent wiggles, alternate the way you change the yarns so that a color change involving no twist is positioned directly above a color change that introduces an extra twist and vice versa. This often happens naturally when you're knitting flat in rows, but you'll want to pay attention to maintaining this alternation when you work in rounds.

Mirrored Patterns

When you switch the colors for a pair of stitches, the knit stitch creates the pattern on one side of the fabric, and the purl stitch creates a mirrored pattern on the other side. Any colorwork or double-knitting pattern would be suitable for this technique.

Argyle, front ◄ | ► *Argyle, back*

ARGYLE

Worked in basic Twigg stitch, this traditional argyle pattern is produced by simply switching the knit and purl colors according to the chart. Doing so creates the same design on both sides, but areas that are light on one side are dark on the other and vice versa.

This swatch was worked with Cascade Yarns 220 Sport (100% wool; 164 yd [150 m]/50 g) in #7827 Goldenrod (yellow; A) and #7824 Jack O'Lantern (orange; B).

NOTES

If working in rows, switch colors on every row by adding an extra twist at the start of the pattern stitches, then return them to their regular positions without a twist. ● If working in rounds, keep the yarns in the same positions for each round. On odd-numbered rounds, switch the colors by adding an extra twist at the start of the pattern stitches, then return them to their regular positions without a twist. On even-numbered rounds, switch the colors without a twist, then return them to their regular positions by adding an extra twist.

Work sts in established Twigg-stitch pattern unless color-switch sts are specified. Exchanging colors as described in the Notes, work as foll:

ROW 1: (knit with A; purl with B) *Work 2 color-switch sts (knit with B; purl with A), work 10 sts as established; rep from * to last 2 sts, work 2 color-switch sts.

ROW 2 AND ALL EVEN-NUMBERED ROWS: (knit with B; purl with A) Work in established rib patt, switching colors to match the sts of the previous row.

ROW 3: (knit with A; purl with B) *Work 2 sts, work 2 color-switch sts, work 6 sts, work 6 color-switch sts, work 6 sts, work 2 color-switch sts; rep from * to last 2 sts, work 2 sts.

ROW 5: (knit with A; purl with B) *Work 4 sts, work 2 color-switch sts, work 2 sts, work 10 color-switch sts, work 2 sts, work 2 color-switch sts, work 2 sts; rep from * to last 2 sts, work 2 sts.

ARGYLE

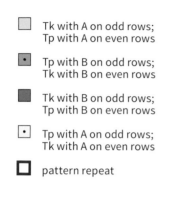

Tk with A on odd rows;
Tp with A on even rows

Tp with B on odd rows;
Tk with B on even rows

Tk with B on odd rows;
Tp with B on even rows

Tp with A on odd rows;
Tk with A on even rows

pattern repeat

mult of 24 sts + 2 and 20 rows + 2

ROW 7: (knit with A; purl with B) *Work 6 sts, work 2 color-switch sts, work 2 sts, work 6 color-switch sts, work 2 sts, work 2 color-switch sts, work 4 sts; rep from * to last 2 sts, work 2 sts.

ROW 9: (knit with A; purl with B) *Work 4 sts, work 6 color-switch sts, work 2 sts, work 2 color-switch sts, work 2 sts, work 6 color-switch sts, work 2 sts; rep from * to last 2 sts, work 2 sts.

ROW 11: (knit with A; purl with B) *Work 2 sts, work 10 color-switch sts; rep from * to last 2 sts, work 2 sts.

ROW 13: Rep Row 9.

ROW 15: Rep Row 7.

ROW 17: Rep Row 5.

ROW 19: Rep Row 3.

ROW 20: (knit with B; purl with A) Work in established rib patt, switching colors to match the sts of Row 19.

Repeat Rows 1–20 for pattern, then work Rows 1 and 2 once more to balance.

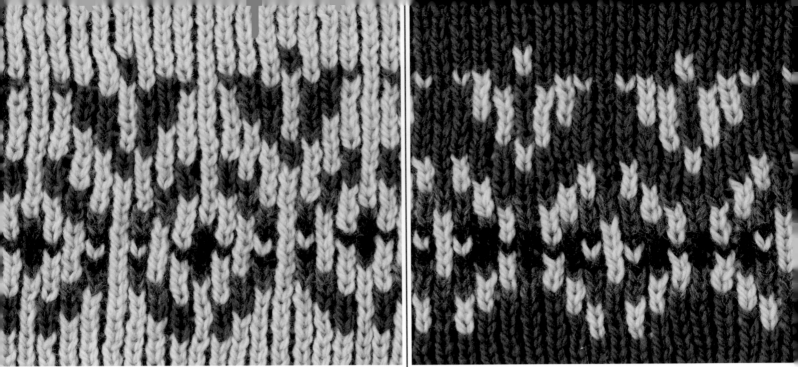

Fair Isle, front ◄ | ► Fair Isle, back

FAIR ISLE

Fair Isle designs worked in Twigg stitch can be especially beautiful when the changing colors on one side are set against a single color on the other to create an added dimension.

This swatch was worked with Cascade Yarns 220 Sport (100% wool; 164 yd [150 m]/50 g) in #9477 Tutu (pink, A), #7818 Blue Velvet (dark blue; B), #2450 Mystic Purple (dark purple; C), #7803 Magenta (dark pink; D), and #8267 Forest Green (dark green; E).

Exchanging colors as described in the Notes, work as foll:

ROW 1: (knit with A; purl with B) *Work 6 sts, work 2 color-switch sts (knit with B; purl with A), work 2 sts, work 2 color-switch sts, work 4 sts; rep from * to last 2 sts, Tk1, Tp1.

ROW 2: (knit with B; purl with A) Work as for Row 1.

ROW 3: (knit with A; purl with B) *Work 4 sts, work 4 color-switch sts, work 2 sts, work 4 color-switch sts, work 2 sts; rep from * to last 2 sts, work 2 sts.

ROW 4: (knit with C; purl with A) *Work 4 sts, work 2 color-switch sts, work 6 sts work 2 color-switch sts, work 2 sts; rep from * to last 2 sts, work 2 sts.

NOTES

If working in rows, switch colors every row by adding an extra twist at the start of the pattern stitches, then return them to their regular positions without a twist. ● If working in rounds, on odd-numbered rounds twist the yarns the same as when working in rows. On even-numbered rounds, switch the colors without a twist and return them to their regular positions by adding an extra twist. ● Work in Twigg-stitch rib throughout. On odd-numbered rows, work the regular stitches using A to knit and B, C, D, or E to purl to create the solid light background; work the pattern in color-switch stitches. On even-numbered rows, work the regular stitches using B, C, D, or E to knit and A to purl for a striped dark background and work color-switch stitches for the pattern.

ROW 5: (knit with A; purl with C) *Work 2 sts, work 4 color-switch sts, work 6 sts, work 4 color-switch sts; rep from * to last 2 sts, work 2 sts.

ROW 6: (knit with C; purl with A) *Work 2 sts, work 2 color-switch sts, work 4 sts, work 2 color-switch sts, work 4 sts, work 2 color-switch sts; rep from * to last 2 sts, work 2 sts.

ROW 7: (knit with A; purl with D) Work as for Row 6.

ROW 8: (knit with D; purl with A) *Work 6 sts, work 6 color-switch sts, work 4 sts; rep from * to last 2 sts, work 2 sts.

ROW 9: (knit with A; purl with D) Work as for Row 6.

ROW 10: (knit with C; purl with A) Work as for Row 6.

ROW 11: (knit with A; purl with C) Work as for Row 5.

ROW 12: (knit with C; purl with A) Work as for Row 4.

ROW 13: (knit with A; purl with B) Work as for Row 3.

ROW 14: (knit with B; purl with A) Work as for Row 2.

ROW 15: (knit with A; purl with B) *Work 2 color-switch sts, work 4 sts, work 2 color-switch sts, work 2 sts, work 2 color-switch sts, work 4 sts; rep from * to last 2 sts, work 2 color-switch sts.

ROW 16: (knit with B; purl with A) *Work 2 color-switch sts, work 14 sts; rep from * to last 2 sts, work 2 color-switch sts.

ROW 17: (knit with A; purl with E) *Work 2 sts, work 2 color-switch sts, work 10 sts, work 2 color-switch sts; rep from * to last 2 sts, work 2 sts.

ROW 18: (knit with E; purl with A) Work as for Row 17.

ROW 19: (knit with A; purl with E) Work as for Row 5.

ROW 20: (knit with E; purl with A) Work as for Row 5.

ROW 21: (knit with A; purl with E) Work as for Row 5.

ROW 22: (knit with E; purl with A) Work as for Row 3.

ROW 23: (knit with A; purl with B) Work as for Row 16.

ROW 24: (knit with B; purl with A) Work as for Row 16.

FAIR ISLE

Tk with A on odd rows; Tp with A on even rows

Tk with B on odd rows; Tp with B on even rows

Tk with C on odd rows; Tp with C on even rows

Tk with D on odd rows; Tp with D on even rows

Tk with E on odd rows; Tp with E on even rows

Tp with A on odd rows; Tk with A on even rows

Tp with B on odd rows; Tk with B on even rows

Tp with C on odd rows; Tk with C on even rows

Tp with D on odd rows; Tk with D on even rows

Tp with E on odd rows; Tk with E on even rows

pattern repeat

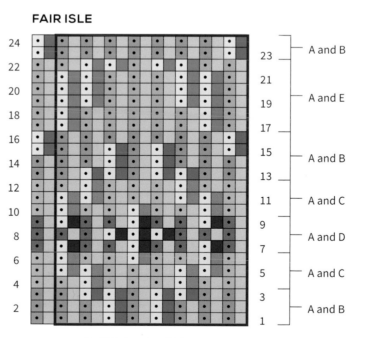

mult of 16 sts + 2 and 24 rows

Bands and Braids

The two-color nature of Twigg stitch makes it ideal for adding simple bands or braids to your knitting. The samples shown here are worked over just a few rows and add eye-catching horizontal elements to the foundation fabric. Use them to decorate the cuff of a mitten, brim of a hat, or edge of a scarf.

All of these examples are shown on a foundation of basic Twigg stitch with the knit stitches worked in the light (A) color and the purl stitches worked in the dark (B) color. Work in basic Twigg stitch to where you want to insert the border or braid, ending with an even-numbered dark-side row. Each pattern begins with an odd-numbered light-side row.

The swatches in this section were worked with Cascade Yarns 220 Sport (100% wool; 164 yd [150 m]/50 g) in #8908 Anis (aqua; A) and #7818 Blue Velvet (dark blue; B).

Mistake Stitch

You can achieve a variety of effects by introducing mistake stitch (see page 112) in a controlled manner. Use two-sided mistake stitch (see box on page 161) for patterns that will look the same on both sides of the fabric, except that the colors will be reversed.

SINGLE HORIZONTAL LINE (EVEN NUMBER OF STS)

This pattern forms a horizontal line of contrasting dashes; the colors are reversed on the back of the fabric.

ROW 1: (knit with A; purl with B) Work two-sided mistake st pattern row (see box on page 161).

ROW 2: (knit with B; purl with A) Work in Twigg st as established.

Continue in Twigg st.

BRICKWORK (MULT OF 4 STS)

This pattern forms somewhat of a checkerboard effect that's worked over a multiple of 4 sts. The colors are reversed on the other side of the fabric.

> **note**: Match the color of the existing sts on all rows.

ROW 1: (knit with A; purl with B) Work two-sided mistake st (see box on page 161).

ROW 2: (knit with B; purl with A) *Work 2 sts in Twigg st, work 2 sts in two-sided mistake st; rep from *.

ROW 3: (knit with A; purl with B) *Work 2 sts in Twigg st, work 2 sts in two-sided mistake st; rep from *.

ROW 4: (knit with B; purl with A) Work two-sided mistake st.

Continue in Twigg st.

DOTTED PATTERN (MULT OF 4 STS)

This pattern forms a band of the contrasting color punctuated with isolated dots of the main color and is worked over a multiple of 4 stitches. The colors are reversed on the back of the fabric.

> **note**: Match the color of the existing sts on all rows.

ROW 1: (knit with A; purl with B) Work two-sided mistake st (see box on page 161).

ROW 2: (knit with B; purl with A) *Work 2 sts in Twigg st, work 2 sts in two-sided mistake st; rep from *.

ROW 3: (knit with A; purl with B) *Work 2 sts in two-sided mistake st, work 2 sts in Twigg st; rep from *.

Mistake Stitch, front. Top to bottom: Single Horizontal Line, ◄
Brickwork, Dotted Pattern, Beaded Pattern, Ribbon Pattern.

► *Mistake Stitch, back. Top to bottom: Single Horizontal Line,*
Brickwork, Dotted Pattern, Beaded Pattern, Ribbon Pattern.

ROW 4: (knit with B; purl with A) Work two-sided mistake st.

Continue in Twigg st.

BEADED PATTERN (EVEN NUMBER OF STS)

This pattern forms a beaded line of the main color centered on a narrow stripe of the contrasting color; the colors are reversed on the back of the fabric.

ROW 1: (knit with B; purl with A) Working each st in the opposite color, work in Twigg st as established.

ROW 2: (knit with A; purl with B) Work two-sided mistake st (see box at right), matching the colors of the existing sts.

Continue in Twigg st, switching the colors back to their original positions (knit with A; purl with B).

RIBBON PATTERN (EVEN NUMBER OF STS)

The narrow stripe of the contrasting color is bordered at the top and bottom with horizontal dashes, one in the contrasting color and the other in the main color; the colors are reversed on the back of the fabric.

ROW 1: (knit with B; purl with A) Working each st in the opposite color, work two-sided mistake st (see box below).

ROW 2: (knit with A; purl with B) Work in Twigg st, matching the colors of the existing sts.

ROW 3: (knit with A; purl with B) Working each st in the opposite color, work two-sided mistake st.

Continue in Twigg st with the even-numbered dark side facing, switching the colors back to their original positions (knit with B; purl with A).

TWO-SIDED MISTAKE STITCH

Pattern row: Work on a Tk1, Tp1 background rib. Hold the knit yarn in back of the work and hold the purl yarn in front of the work and operate the right needle between the two yarns. *Knit 1 regular stitch with the knit yarn, purl 1 regular stitch with the purl yarn; rep from *, using the colors as directed.

Garter Stitch, front. Top to bottom: Single Ridge With Same ◄
Color, Single Ridge With Contrast Color, Combination Ridge,
Single Ridge With Mixed Colors, Double Ridge With Mixed Colors.

► Garter Stitch, back. Top to bottom: Single Ridge With Same Color,
Single Ridge With Contrast Color, Combination Ridge, Single
Ridge With Mixed Colors, Double Ridge With Mixed Colors.

Garter Stitch

Garter-stitch ridges are essentially lines of reversed
double knitting. To create this simple effect, hold
one yarn in front in the purl position and the other
in back in the knit position. Use the right needle
to work between the two yarns, purling the knit
stitches with the yarn held in front and knitting
the purl stitches with the yarn held in back. The
patterns look the same on both sides of the fabric,
except that the colors are reversed.

All of these examples are shown on a foundation
of basic Twigg stitch with the knit stitches worked
in the light (A) color and the purl stitches worked
in the dark (B) color.

SINGLE RIDGE WITH SAME COLOR

This pattern forms a simple garter ridge of the main color;
the colors are reversed on the back of the fabric.

PATTERN ROW: Holding A in front and B in back and
matching the colors of the existing sts, *purl 1 regular st
with A, knit 1 regular st with B; rep from *.

Continue in Twigg st with the even-numbered dark side
facing and switching the knits and purls back to their
original positions (knit with B; purl with A).

SINGLE RIDGE WITH CONTRAST COLOR

Here, the garter ridge is in the contrasting color. The pattern is worked over 2 rows so that the top and bottom bumps of the garter ridge are the same color; the colors are reversed on the back of the fabric.

ROW 1: (knit with B; purl with A) Working each st in the opposite color, work in Twigg st.

ROW 2: Holding A in front and B in back, and matching the colors of the existing sts, *purl 1 regular st with A, knit 1 regular st with B; rep from *.

Continue in Twigg st, switching the colors back to their original positions.

COMBINATION RIDGE

In this variation, a garter ridge of the main color sits above a garter ridge of the contrasting color with a Twigg-stitch row in between; the colors are reversed on the back of the fabric.

ROW 1: (knit with B; purl with A) Working each st in the opposite color, work in Twigg st.

ROW 2: Holding A in front and B in back, and matching the colors of the existing sts, *purl 1 regular st with A, knit 1 regular st with B; rep from *.

ROW 3: (knit with A; purl with B) Working each st in the opposite color, work in Twigg st.

ROW 4: Holding B in front and A in back, and matching the colors of the existing sts, *purl 1 regular st with B, knit 1 regular st with A; rep from *.

Resume working in Twigg st, matching the colors of the existing sts.

SINGLE RIDGE WITH MIXED COLORS

For this version, the lower bumps of the ridge are in the contrasting color, and the upper bumps are in the main color; the colors are reversed on the back of the fabric.

PATTERN ROW: Holding B in front and A in back, and working each st in the opposite color, *purl 1 regular st with B, knit 1 regular st with A; rep from *.

Continue in Twigg st with the even-numbered dark side facing, switching the colors and the knit and purl sts back to their original positions (knit with B; purl with A).

DOUBLE RIDGE WITH MIXED COLORS

This variation has two mixed-color garter ridges in which the colors are mirrored. Of the four lines of bumps, the two middle lines will be in the main color. The colors are reversed on the back of the fabric.

ROW 1: Holding B in front and A in back, and working each st in the opposite color, *purl 1 regular st with B, knit 1 regular st with A; rep from *.

ROW 2: (knit with A; purl with B) Work in Twigg st, matching the colors of the existing sts.

ROW 3: Holding A in front and B in back, and working each st in the opposite color, *purl 1 regular st with A, knit 1 regular st with B; rep from *.

Continue in Twigg st with the even-numbered dark side facing, matching the colors of the existing sts (knit with B; purl with A).

Latvian braid, front. Top to bottom: Single Line With ◄
Matching Colors, Double Line With Matching Colors,
Double-Line Variation With Matching Colors, Single Line
With Reversed Colors, Double Line With Reversed Colors.

► *Latvian braid, back. Top to bottom: Single Line With*
Matching Colors, Double Line With Matching Colors,
Double-Line Variation With Matching Colors, Single Line
With Reversed Colors, Double Line With Reversed Colors.

Latvian Braids

Latvian braids form twisted two-color bands on the surface of knitted fabrics; they're often used to decorate the cuffs of mittens or the brims of hats. Traditionally, the braids are formed by rows of purl stitches worked on a stockinette-stitch background, but when worked over two rows in Twigg stitch, the braid appears on both sides, so all the stitches can be knitted if desired. When working in the round, alternate a round of knit stitches with a round of purl stitches or vice versa.

The braid effect is formed by alternating the colors every stitch and twisting the two yarns around each other as you go. To ensure that all of the twists slant in the same direction, take care to exchange the yarns consistently across the row—always bringing the new yarn either over the old or under the old.

You can create some quite interesting effects by varying the direction of the twists on successive braid rows, by either matching the colors of the existing stitches (as in the first three braid patterns) or contrasting the stitch colors (as in the last two patterns).

SINGLE LINE WITH MATCHING COLORS

The simplest form of the braid creates matching twisted lines on each side of the fabric. The twists slant in the opposite direction on the back of the fabric.

ROW 1: Holding one yarn at a time (see box at right) and matching the colors of the existing sts, *knit 1 regular st with A, knit 1 regular st with B; rep from *, always bringing the new color up in back of the old color.

ROW 2: Holding one yarn at a time and matching the colors of the existing sts, *knit 1 regular st with B, knit 1 regular st with A; rep from *, always bringing the new color up in front of the old color to untwist the yarns.

Continue in Twigg st.

DOUBLE LINE WITH MATCHING COLORS

This pattern is a double version of the single line with matching colors, one that produces a more pronounced diagonal effect. The twists slant in the opposite direction on the back of the fabric.

ROWS 1 AND 3: Work as for Row 1 of Single Line with Matching Colors.

ROWS 2 AND 4: Work as for Row 2 of Single Line with Matching Colors.

Continue in Twigg st.

DOUBLE-LINE VARIATION WITH MATCHING COLORS

This pattern begins with the same first 2 rows as the Single or Double Line with Matching Colors, then the yarns twist in the opposite direction on the following 2 rows to create a chevron effect. The V of the chevron points in the opposite direction on the back of the fabric.

ROW 1: Holding one yarn at a time (see box below) and matching the colors of the existing sts, *knit 1 regular st with A, knit 1 regular st with B; rep from *, always bringing the new color up in back of the old color.

ROW 2: Holding one yarn at a time and matching the colors of the existing sts, *knit 1 regular st with B, knit 1 regular st with A; rep from *, always bringing the new color up in front of the old color to untwist the yarns.

ROW 3: Holding one yarn at a time and matching the colors of the existing sts, *knit 1 regular st with A, knit 1 regular st with B; rep from *, always bringing the new color up in front of the old color.

ROW 4: Holding one yarn at a time and matching the colors of the existing sts, *knit 1 regular st with B, knit 1 regular st with A; rep from *, always bringing the new color up in back of the old color to untwist the yarns.

Continue in Twigg st.

SINGLE LINE WITH REVERSED COLORS

Using the opposite colors for each stitch creates a different effect. The twists slant in the opposite direction on the back of the fabric.

ROW 1: Holding one yarn at a time (see box below) and working each st in the opposite color, *knit 1 regular st with B, knit 1 regular st with A; rep from *, always bringing the new color up in back of the old color.

ROW 2: Holding one yarn at a time and working each st in the opposite color, *knit 1 regular st with B, knit 1 regular st with A; rep from *, always bringing the new color up in front of the old color to untwist the yarns.

Continue in Twigg st.

DOUBLE LINE WITH REVERSED COLORS

Working the single line with reversed colors twice in succession makes a braid that looks somewhat like a band of embroidery stitches across the knitting. The twists slant in the opposite direction on the back of the fabric.

Rows 1 and 3: Work as for Row 1 of Single Line with Reversed Colors.

Rows 2 and 4: Work as for Row 2 of Single Line with Reversed Colors.

Continue in Twigg st.

WORKING WITH ONE YARN AT A TIME

To work with one yarn at a time, select the color to use for the first stitch, work the stitch, then drop this color. Bring the new color up either in back of the old color or in front of the old color as specified, work the next stitch, then drop the new color. Continue in the same manner, alternating colors and creating a twist between the yarns as you bring the new color into position after each stitch. The working yarns will get twisted around each other quite a lot between the knitting and the balls of yarn, but you will untwist them on the following row.

SOURCES FOR SUPPLIES

BROWN SHEEP COMPANY

100662 County Rd. 16
Mitchell, NE 69357
brownsheep.com

CASCADE YARNS

PO Box 58168
1224 Andover Park East
Tukwila, WA 98188
cascadeyarns.com

**FAIRMONT FIBERS/
MANOS DEL URUGUAY**

PO Box 2082
Philadelphia, PA 19103
fairmountfibers.com

MALABRIGO

malabrigoyarn.com

O-WOOL

915 N. 28th St.
Philadelphia, PA 19130
o-wool.com

SHIBUI KNITS

1500 NW 18th St. Ste. 110
Portland, OR 97209
shibuiknits.com

INDEX

EXPAND YOUR GARMENT AND ACCESSORIES WARDROBE

with these knitting resources from Interweave

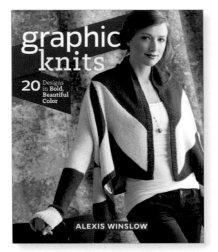

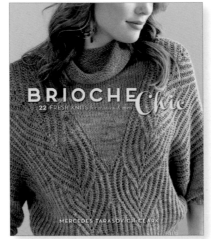

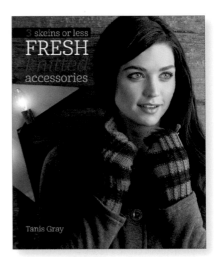

GRAPHIC KNITS
20 Designs in Bold,
Beautiful Color

Alexis Winslow

ISBN 978-1-62033-126-2, $24.99

BRIOCHE CHIC
22 Fresh Knits
for Women & Men

Mercedes Tarasovich-Clark

ISBN 978-1-62033-442-3, $26.99

3 SKEINS OR LESS:
**FRESH KNITTED
ACCESSORIES**

Tanis Gray

ISBN 978-1-62033-673-1, $24.99